NATO: Its Past, Present, and Future

Peter Duignan

NATO:
Its Past, Present, and Future

Hoover Institution Press   Stanford University   Stanford, California

355
DUI

www-hoover.org

Hoover Institution Press Publication No. 470

Copyright © 2000 by the Board of Trustees of the
  Leland Stanford Junior University

First printing, 2000

Manufactured in the United States of America

06 05 04 03 02   9 8 7 6 5 4 3 2

The paper used in this publication meets the minimum requirements of
American National Standard for Information Sciences—Permanence of
Paper for Printed Library Materials, ANSI Z39.48-1984.

Cover photos: NATO soldiers, © Reuters NewMedia Inc./Corbis;
NATO flag, © Artville; background, © PhotoDisc

Library of Congress Cataloging-in-Publication Data
Duignan, Peter.
  NATO: its past, present, and future / by Peter Duignan.
    p. cm.
  Includes bibliographical references and index.
  ISBN 0-8179-9782-2 (alk. paper)
    1. North Atlantic Treaty Organization—History.   I. Title.
UA646.3.D818 2000
355'.031091821—dc21   00-029567

Contents

Maps

Preface

The purpose of this book is to look at the fifty-year history of NATO (1949–1999), the most successful alliance system in the history of the world. NATO protected Western Europe from communism and brought the West together in the Atlantic Alliance—an alliance system that made war impossible between twelve nations that had gone to war with each other twice previously in the twentieth century. The NATO shield allowed Europe's economy to recover and grow and democracy to return to Germany and Italy. NATO had three purposes: to keep the Russians out, the Germans down, and the Americans in Europe. Although the Cold War is over, Russia still remains a potential threat to the region. The Europeans still need to be reassured by the continued involvement of the United States in controlling Germany and in extending protection to the new members of NATO, Poland, Hungary, the Czech Republic, and nations even further into Eastern Europe.

Born in 1949 as the Cold War began, NATO evolved from a warfighting, defensive alliance that kept the peace in Europe until the war broke out in Bosnia-Herzegovina in the 1990s. NATO had become a force for peacekeeping and conciliation after the breakup of the Warsaw Pact (1989) and then was drawn into a war against Yugoslavia. So significant was the war in Kosovo that I decided to extend the coverage beyond 1999 and follow that crucial event in NATO's history into the year 2000. The air war over Serbia and Kosovo, and the occupation of Kosovo by NATO forces (KFOR), created a new NATO, perhaps one with a new interventionist strategy for the future. NATO had been a defensive alliance for Western

Europe during the Cold War and then a peacekeeper after 1990. But then, in a seventy-eight-day air war, it bombed Yugoslavia, a sovereign state, for mistreating its citizens in one of its provinces, Kosovo. The change in NATO's behavior will have vast consequences for the United States and its NATO allies.

Since the end of the Cold War, NATO has been looking for a reason for its continued existence. The humanitarian intervention in Kosovo may become that raison d'être. Although international law said that external aggression should be resisted, no such right exists to intervene in the internal affairs of a sovereign nation. The implications for the future are stark. What will NATO do against Russia, China, and India if internal conflicts develop in those nations?

The conduct of the Kosovo war also divided NATO, weakened U.S. control over the alliance, and stimulated the EU to develop an independent European Security and Defense Identity (ESDI) with its own rapid reaction force and military-industrial complex. This could weaken the U.S. resolve to stay in NATO and to act as Europe's defensive shield. All this is in stark contrast with the first fifty years of NATO, when NATO was a successful military alliance dominated by the United States. This essay charts the years from 1949 to 1999, and beyond, to look into the future to see what NATO might become in the twenty-first century.

I want to thank my Hoover colleagues Thomas Henriksen and James Morrow for reading and commenting on the manuscript, as well as Harold Farmer who typed and checked facts, figures, and the organization of the manuscript. I alone, however, am responsible for the interpretation and any flaws and errors. In addition, I would like to acknowledge the support of John Raisian, director of the Hoover Institution, for encouraging me to do this book on NATO under the Hoover program on International Rivalries and Global Cooperation. Also I wish to express my gratitude to Pat Baker, executive editor of the Hoover Press, and the staff at the Hoover Press for their efforts in publishing this work on NATO's history and future.

Part I

The Origins of NATO, 1949–1960

Harry S. Truman became the thirty-third president of the United States after the death of President Franklin D. Roosevelt on April 12, 1945. Truman had had very little experience in foreign affairs, but was aided by Secretaries of State George C. Marshall and Dean Acheson, and other officials in the Department of State, such as George Kennan and Charles Bohlen. Truman's first major foreign-policy decision was to drop atomic bombs to end the Pacific War and to restrain the Soviet Union. It was, however, as a leader in the Cold War that Truman will be ranked high in history's pantheon of great leaders.

At war's end Truman had demobilized over twelve million persons in the armed services and, in effect, pulled out of Europe. Good relations with the Soviet Union proved impossible. When a weakened Britain decided in 1947 to withdraw from the Eastern Mediterranean, Greece was left alone to fight a Soviet-backed civil war, and Turkey was also threatened by the Soviet Union. President Truman, on March 12, 1947, then announced the Truman Doctrine (written by Truman and Under Secretary of State Dean Acheson) to give immediate economic and military aid to Greece and Turkey in a first effort to resist Soviet expansionism. The U.S. Congress responded to Truman's message by appropriating $400 million to save Greece and Turkey. Thus was born the policy of containment—but it was not limited to military aid in the eastern Mediterranean. Under the European Recovery Program (the Marshall Plan, 1947–51), Truman offered economic aid to help Europe rebuild and recover from the ravages of World War II. In 1948 Congress buttressed the Marshall Plan by creating the Economic Cooperation Administration (ECA) to help create a common market in Western Europe, to assist in restoring the economies of Europe and thus enable them to better resist the Soviet Union and its allies.

The Birth of NATO

In Europe itself, Britain, France, Belgium, the Netherlands, and Luxembourg formed the Western European Union (WEU), to prevent either Germany or the USSR from dominating Europe. Because of the Berlin Blockade (1948) and Communist aggression in Czechoslovakia and Korea, the United States and the WEU combined forces in a new alliance, the North Atlantic Treaty Organization (1949).

Early in 1950, President Truman set up a working group from the National Security Council, the State Department, and the Department of Defense to study national security policy. This group produced the landmark National Security Council (NSC) Memorandum 68, which called for a massive conventional military buildup and a global system of alliances—NATO, SEATO, and the United States–Japan Security Treaty. Yet Truman did little and called for yet another study. (It was only after North Korea invaded South Korea on June 25, 1950, that NSC Memorandum 68 became operational to carry out Truman's policies of containment in Asia and to arm NATO.) After 1951, economic aid through the Marshall Plan was transformed into military aid to equip NATO and, in 1954, to rearm West Germany to be NATO's military shield against the Soviet Union.

Truman thus reversed the traditional isolationism of the United States, returning troops to Europe in NATO in 1950–51 under General Dwight Eisenhower, then rearming West Germany and thus reconciling World War II enemies and friends. In 1951 Allied Command Europe became operational, with Supreme Headquarters Allied Powers Europe (SHAPE) located at Roquemcourt, near Paris. The United States, under Truman, helped rebuild the economies of Western Europe, and kept itself involved in European affairs, resulting in fifty years of peace, stability, and economic growth, the "golden years" of modern European history. NATO formed, and continued to form, the most successful peacetime venture in Western cooperation. The alliance lasted much longer than its architects had anticipated; it also developed into a more integrated political and military organization than its makers had planned.

Not that NATO lacked blemishes. It suffered from internal jealousies and disputes, but such deficiencies were at least partially balanced by the fact that the NATO partners freely cooperated in a common endeavor—unlike those of the Eastern Bloc consolidated through the formation of Comecon (Council for Mutual Economic Assistance) set up on June 25, 1949, and the Warsaw Pact, concluded on May 14, 1955.

NATO, in fact, was a purely defensive alliance to protect Western Europe and was not able or willing to project its power anywhere else. (Initially, the Allies had planned to withdraw behind the Rhine; but once the West Germans were admitted in 1954, NATO switched to "forward defense" that would avoid surrendering the bulk of the Federal Republic to the invaders.) NATO was also defensive in a purely political sense. It lacked a propaganda or political warfare branch. NATO was not framed to exploit what Lenin would have called "internal contradictions." Of these there were many within the Soviet empire—the contradictions between the needs of rigid central planning and growing consumer demands, between the hegemonical power of the Soviet Union and the dependent Communist regimes, between the ethnic groups within the Soviet Union, between the regnant Marxist-Leninist philosophy and popular religious beliefs. NATO policymakers did not try to embarrass the

Soviet Union politically, say, by calling for the independence of the Baltic republics, former sovereign states and members of the League of Nations but now absorbed by the Soviet Union. NATO policy-makers were content with "containment." Even "containment" came under fire, as George F. Kennan, the man who first coined the phrase, spent much of his subsequent career criticizing his brain-child as being too militaristic in its implementation, when he had called for the political containment of communism. From the po-litical warfare perspective, Western policy remained reactive. The troubles experienced by the Soviet Union within its own sphere re-mained uncovenanted benefits, apples that dropped from a tree that NATO policymakers proved reluctant to shake. The formation of NATO nevertheless represented a turning point in the history, both of the United States and of the Atlantic powers as a whole. For the first time in peacetime, the United States had engaged in a perma-nent alliance linking itself to Western Europe in both a military and a political sense.

Opposition to NATO continued, from Communist states, old-style isolationists, pacifists, the pro-Communist left and, later on, from the new right. But NATO's foundations were well laid. Presi-dent Truman, at a critical time, found himself well served by a team of loyal civilian advisers (Acheson, Bohlen, Harriman, Kennan, Lovett, McCloy), men who had gone to expensive prep schools and to prestigious Eastern universities, who believed in public service, and who felt convinced that the United States had a duty to serve the world. Equally important was the new group of soldier statesmen and soldier viceroys—especially Generals MacArthur, Marshall, Lu-cius Clay (military governor in Germany 1947–49), and—on the British side, Sir Gerald Templer (first Director of Civil Affairs and Military Government in the British zone). Clay and Templer be-tween them can rightly claim to be counted among the unacknowl-edged founding fathers of the German Federal Republic.

The success attained by U.S. policymakers went beyond merely personal factors—the statesmanship shown by Truman and his advisers, and the solidity evinced at the time by the so-called Eastern Establishment. Policymakers drew on a mood of profound national confidence at the time when a victorious United States dominated the world militarily, politically, and economically. On the European side, there was also widespread commitment, especially among veterans and college-educated youth, the very group most widely inclined to criticize NATO a generation later. To those who had experienced war and its aftermath, the creation of transnational institutions represented a challenge—especially to those tired of traditional chauvinist slogans.

A year after the North Atlantic Treaty was signed, the British held a conference in London in 1950 which laid out the basic policy objectives for Great Britain: the need to sustain Britain's position as a great power, albeit of the second rank; the higher direction of the Cold War; the necessity to develop and extend Atlantic rather than European institutions of cooperation between Western states; and the transformation of the "special relationship" into a more effective partnership with U.S. Cold War strategy.

The founding of NATO had had unintended consequences. The "special relationship" between Britain and the United States deteriorated. This relationship had depended on the success of the wartime alliance, on Churchill's personal prestige, on the skill displayed by British diplomacy in creating for a time the illusion of Britain's enduring great-power status after World War II. The "special relationship" was sustained also by ties of personal friendship. (For example, Socialist Bevin and General Marshall, an incongruous pair, got on extremely well together.) In a profounder sense, the "special relationship" was supported by a common cultural heritage that linked many British and U.S. diplomats, senior civil servants, and some Establishment politicians.

A good many Britons, for their part, had transatlantic family connections and felt at home in the United States. These ties did not disappear, but within the framework of NATO's high command, Britain counted for less than she had in World War II within SHAEF (Supreme Headquarters, Allied Expeditionary Forces). By the beginning of the 1950s, there was an end to serious discussions concerning an English-speaking union that would comprise the United States, Britain, and the "white" British dominions. By contrast, NATO was a political boon to West Germany and Italy. For both of them, membership in NATO and other transnational bodies meant a new acceptance abroad, and a new political legitimacy. The United States gave up on France as the bulwark of NATO and chose West Germany as the key to NATO's defense and Western Europe's recovery.

The Shaky Balance

The Communists responded to this series of events with a welter of vigorous counteroffensives that blended military power, diplomacy, propaganda, and disinformation in the accustomed fashion. The Soviets detonated their first atomic bomb (announced August 29, 1949), thereby breaking the U.S. nuclear monopoly much more quickly than U.S. experts had anticipated. At the same time, the Cominform (Communist Information Bureau) called for massive efforts from its associate parties to strive against Western rearmament, and to strengthen the Communist position in Western trade unions, youth organizations, women's leagues, and other bodies. The Communists' political effort in Western Europe, however, did not fare well. Communist strategists had assumed that a series of economic crises and strikes would make Western Europe increasingly vulnerable in a political sense. Instead, the Western economies expanded in a dramatic fashion so that the Western Communist parties increasingly found themselves mere bystanders in a drama that failed to conform to the Marxist-Leninist script.

Above all, the Communists failed in their primary endeavor—to prevent West Germany's integration into NATO. West German rearmament at first proceeded slowly. The process began in May 1950 when Adenauer created the *Zentrale für Heimatdienst* as a secret think tank to study rearmament. In the next month, however, North Korean forces invaded South Korea. The United States suddenly found itself involved in a major war, and became an ardent advocate of German rearmament.*

Truman finally went for a global strategy in 1950 after reading a National Security Council Report (NSC Memorandum 68) about a Soviet atomic weapon explosion in August 1949. This, coupled with Mao's victory in China (1949), led to a new global strategy for the United States. The Soviets were seen to have become more than a political menace, for with atomic weapons they threatened to conquer the world by piecemeal aggression. The "domino theory" emerged, calling on the United States to resist all Communist adventures. When the North Koreans attacked in 1950, the United States rallied the United Nations to oppose this aggression. As noted previously, NATO's military wing was organized and armed in 1951–52 by the North Atlantic Council Organization, to make NATO a permanent organization, headquartered in Paris. General Eisenhower became the Supreme Commander in Europe. Stalin died on March 26, 1953; two days later the North Koreans agreed to the United Nations Repatriation Commission. In May 1954 the

---

*In May 1945 the U.S. Army in Western Europe numbered 3,500,000; by March 1946 only 400,000 troops remained, and even after the Truman Doctrine (1947) and the policy of containment were in place, troop strength in Europe was reduced even further until it numbered 81,000 in 1950, even after the formation of NATO in 1949—hardly the kind of force an aggressive, anti-Communist power would have deployed.

USSR made a bid to join NATO but was rejected by the United States and the United Kingdom.

Stalin's death, war weariness, and the threat of U.S. nuclear weapons had brought the Chinese and the Russians to Panmunjom. Some critics claim that the United States made a great mistake in using the UN to defend Korea because this harmed that body's role as a peacekeeping force. This writer would argue quite the contrary; it exposed Communist bloc expansionism, showed the resolve and effectiveness of resisting aggression by collective action, and thereby strengthened the hand of world peace through the UN, as opposed to peace through national alliances. A year later, in October 1954, the Federal German Republic formally joined the Western Union, and NATO, and in 1955 formally opened diplomatic relations with the USSR. To counter West Germany's addition to Western power, the Communists strengthened the regime in the Soviet zone by creating the *Kasernierte Volkspolizei*, an armed force composed of regulars (later the nucleus of the *Nationale Volksarmee*, the East German Army). The Soviets also tightened control over the captive "bourgeois" parties within their zone.

The Warsaw Pact profited by driving a neutral wedge between the northern and southern segments of NATO. There was a brief lull in the Cold War, soon broken by the Soviets' repression of the Hungarian uprising (1956), and by the Soviets' new use of "atomic diplomacy" against Britain and France during the Suez crisis. (In 1956 Britain and France cooperated with Israel in an attempt to seize the Suez Canal, a venture that failed when the United States sided with the Arabs and the Soviet Union against its Western allies.)

Secretary of State John Foster Dulles called for a "rollback" of Soviet power, but in fact he did nothing over Hungary; the United States lacked the resources to do anything effective. It was rather British power that was rolled back; the British retreat in 1956 in turn created new opportunities for the Soviet Union in the Middle East. Although Dulles had at first believed in accommodation with the

Soviet Union, by 1952 he feared a dynamic Soviet communism and felt containment was too passive a policy to combat Soviet militarism. He saw the need to win more cooperation from the Europeans and to organize regional pacts to restrain the Soviets; yet Dulles soon recognized the United States had limited resources to sustain global hegemony. With President Eisenhower and the National Security Council he developed a new grand strategy — beyond mere containment — of massive retaliation to aggression.

NATO was pressured to assume more burdens. Although the United States took on more and more foreign responsibilities, Eisenhower as president cut the military budget for conventional arms and decided to depend for deterrence on nuclear weapons. In this the United States yielded to pressure from its NATO allies who did not want to spend large sums on conventional weaponry instead of on welfare programs. Earlier the North Atlantic Council had met in Boston in 1952 and called for the buildup of conventional forces; but it recognized that these forces could not be paid for and chose to rely on nuclear deterrence instead.

Dulles had responded to the Soviet threat by building a series of NATO-like regional pacts (begun by Acheson in 1951 with ANZUS to protect the Pacific Basin), as well as CENTRO (Central Treaty Organization with Turkey, Iran, and Pakistan, 1959) and SEATO (South East Asian Treaty Organization, 1957). But when the United States failed to counter the Soviet suppression in Hungary in 1956, Dulles's policy lost much credibility, at least outwardly.

NATO: Organization and Strategy

"NATO is an organization of sovereign nations equal in status" proclaims NATO's own handbook. A more inaccurate statement would be hard to find, even in official handouts. From its beginnings in 1949, NATO was characterized by the diversity of its membership.

The founder states comprised Belgium, Canada, Denmark, France, Iceland, Italy, Luxembourg, the Netherlands, Norway, Portugal, the United Kingdom, and the United States—joined in 1952 by Greece and Turkey, two hostile allies, and in 1954 by the Federal German Republic. There was an enormous disparity of power and status between its members—with the United States on the one extreme of the spectrum, and Norway and Iceland on the other.

Critics of the alliance were fond of censuring it as no more than a façade concealing an "American protectorate in Europe."[1] The United States in fact remained immeasurably superior to its allies in nuclear weaponry and economic strength. (By 1953, the 176 million North Americans still accounted for a total economic output about three times that attained by the 208 million citizens of the European NATO states.) The United States, moreover, made great sacrifices in resisting Communist aggression in Korea. (The U.S. forces incurred 157,000 casualties, about 95 percent of those suffered by the sixteen participating members. More than $15 billion were spent by the United States on the war. These sacrifices were soon forgotten.) But the United States at any rate had demonstrated its willingness to support a threatened ally. Henceforth there would be no more talk about "Americans willing to fight to the last allied soldier."

Primacy within the NATO alliance of necessity therefore fell to the United States. Nevertheless, NATO—unlike the Warsaw Pact—rested on its members' free consent, even that of the weakest. It was NATO's character as a voluntary association that constituted both its weakness and its strength. None of its European members wanted to experience once more the agonies either of occupation or of liberation. The NATO alliance might not have engendered enthusiasm; but it rested on popular support.

NATO's supreme command inevitably passed to the United States. (Indeed, NATO's very foundation implied a steady decline in the "special relationship" that had hitherto existed between Britain and the United States.) In 1950 Eisenhower became the first supreme allied commander (1950–52); it was his personality and prestige that dominated NATO during its first crucial years. Eisenhower, like his functionaries in NATO and his opponents in the Warsaw Pact headquarters, continued to think of the World War II experience. Eisenhower himself was personally acquainted with most of NATO's leading officers. He also profited from the organizational structure set up for the military under the Western Union's auspices. (Its Commanders-in-Chief Defense Committee had formed the first instance of continuous military cooperation and planning in Western Europe in peacetime. But the committee had been beset by bitter rivalry between Lord Montgomery, the chairman, and General Lattre de Tassigny, both brilliant but vainglorious men, with fine war records, and both national heros.) The Western European headquarters at Fontainebleau became the model for Eisenhower's Supreme Headquarters (SHAPE). In Paris, in a like manner, the Western European Military Supply Board was absorbed into NATO's Military Production and Supply Board; the Western European Finance and Economic Committee became the core of NATO's Financial and Economic Board.

NATO's formation created a host of new problems that paralleled those faced in the creation of a Western European association. NATO, according to its critics, was dominated by the "Anglo-Saxons." (Its very designation, "North Atlantic Treaty Organization," took no account of its Mediterranean members.)

The 1948 Berlin blockade also had the unintended effect of strengthening U.S. military commitments to the defense of Europe. Recent works on the origins of the North Atlantic Treaty Alliance dispose of revisionist interpretations according to which NATO was somehow imposed on its European allies by a bellicose United States obsessed with Cold War fantasies. Considerable opposition in fact remained at the time within the U.S. governmental machinery toward permanent European commitments. Many U.S. leaders would have been content to give no more than general support to the Brussels Treaty (signed on March 17, 1947, between Britain, France, and the Benelux countries). But on their own, the forces of the resultant Western Union alliance would clearly have been inadequate.

Western Union, moreover, placed a disproportionately heavy burden of defense on an ailing Great Britain. Ernest Bevin, in consequence, saw the Brussels Treaty and Western Union as "a sprat to catch a whale"—"a device to lure the Americans into giving Western Europe full military backing . . . in much the same way as the joint Western European response to the Marshall Plan offer had procured U.S. economic aid."[2] According to Paul-Henri Spaak, the Belgian foreign minister and another of NATO's architects, the new Washington Treaty would become on the Atlantic scale what the Brussels Treaty—that is to say, Western Union—was on the European scale. Skillful British, Canadian, and Benelux diplomacy thus played a major part in getting the United States to commit herself to an Atlantic alliance. The preamble to the North Atlantic Treaty Organization documents in 1949 stated that the Atlantic community was determined "to safeguard the freedom, common heritage and civilization of their people founded on the principles of democracy, individual liberty and the rule of law."

English became NATO's unofficial language. Traditional national jurisdictions had to be modified through complex arrangements that allowed aircraft, trucks, pipelines, and various communications systems to cross national borders without hindrance. The allies had to coordinate policies and strategy through a supranational organization.

To meet these problems, the allies set up an organization of considerable complexity. The North Atlantic Council served as the supreme organ of the alliance, with permanent representation from each member government. The Council was responsible for implementing the provisions of the treaty; its work was organized by the secretary-general who directed its Secretariat and its six divisions: Political Affairs, Defense Planning and Policy, Defense Support, Infrastructure, Logistics and Council Operations, and Scientific Affairs. The Council's chief administrative officer was the secretary-general. The first incumbent was Lord Ismay, a British general who had made his reputation as chief of staff to the British Minister of Defence during World War II. Ismay held the post until 1957 when he was succeeded by Paul-Henri Spaak, the veteran advocate of a united Europe and—like Eisenhower—a chairman to the manner born.

The Council was assisted by a host of specialized committees and specialized agencies that dealt with matters as diverse as the press services, economics, and such like. NATO's military direction lay with the Military Committee composed of the chief of staff of each member state. Subordinate to the Military Committee were the major commands and planning groups: Supreme Command Europe (SACEUR); Supreme Allied Commander Atlantic (SACLANT); Allied Commander-in-Chief Channel (CINCHAN); Canada–U.S. Regional Planning Group (CUSRPG); and a number of other military agencies. Supreme headquarters were located in Paris, and later shifted to Brussels in 1966 when France withdrew from NATO. (Here NATO's impact, however, was much smaller than the EEC's. By 1987 there were still fewer than 2,300 NATO officials in Brussels, as opposed to 14,000 Eurocrats.) Subordinate agencies were located in Paris, Bonn, and Rome.

NATO remained an association of sovereign nation states; its members could leave the alliance as they pleased. (As noted above, in 1966 France withdrew from NATO's military command, though France continued to cooperate with the alliance; SHAPE moved to Casteau near Mons, Belgium.) Individual members remained free to decide the percentage of their GNP or the size and composition of the forces to be contributed to the alliance. NATO's strength would continue to depend on the power of its national components. NATO's sphere of action remained confined to Western Europe. Threats to the alliance that might emerge elsewhere, in Africa, the

Middle East, or the Caribbean, would still have to be dealt with by its individual members. NATO possessed no coordinated intelligence service; the intelligence services of the individual countries would continue to operate in an uneasy and often mutually hostile fraternity.

NATO lacked a propaganda organization capable of rivaling the Soviet propaganda machine in Western Europe. NATO likewise had no agency for political warfare. In this regard, the allies differed among themselves and individual member states—including the United States—pursued no consistent policy. The want of a coordinated political strategy became all the more obvious during the later 1950s and 1960s when the Soviets became increasingly skillful in their foreign policy, increasingly able to use "peace" slogans on their own behalf, and ever more resolved to make their weight felt in the Third World. The NATO powers, by contrast, were apt to underplay the political dimension of the struggle. Not for them the sound advice given to the Spartans by Alcibiades, most illustrious of Athenian exiles: "The surest way of harming an enemy is to find out certainly what form of attack he is most frightened of and then to employ it against him."[3]

NATO had other weaknesses. NATO proved much less adept at standardizing its equipment than did the Warsaw Pact. NATO's command structure was so complex as to be certain of being superseded in the event of war. NATO continued to be beset by those weaknesses that have traditionally beset all alliances: jealousies, disputes, and burden-sharing debates. NATO's military planners, like their opposite numbers in the Warsaw Pact, continued to think of a future conflict in terms of World War II when they had gained experience, honors, and victory. (Their preoccupation with World War II was shared by the reading public on both sides of the Iron Curtain, a public that continued with enthusiasm to buy war books of every kind.) NATO strategists in particular drew heavily on the air strategy of World War II, now rendered more potent by nuclear arms.

According to the Soviets and their sympathizers, NATO merely represented "the newest form of aggressive capitalism that could only perpetuate itself by embarking on new and ever more threatening imperialist ventures."[4] The Soviet Union was supposedly being encircled by a worldwide system of air bases; Soviet strategy was essentially defensive; NATO's strategy allegedly heightened those perils that it wished to avoid. In this writer's opinion, there was no merit in this argument. Moscow's policy toward the West was not of the kind that befitted a weaker power fearing assault. Soviet strategy put its trust in a sustained offensive that emphasized deception, speed, surprise, and the unremitting use of the strategic initiative. Soviet propaganda, far from conciliatory toward the West, took recourse in unbridled mendacity. The Soviets continued to call for the destruction of capitalism worldwide. The Soviets unhesitatingly challenged the Allies' position in West Berlin; the Soviets openly supported North Korean aggression. Soviet policy toward the West during the 1950s strikingly contrasted with Stalin's during the two years preceding the German attack against Russia, when the Soviets genuinely feared German aggression, and attempted a policy of peaceful coexistence with the Third Reich.

NATO strategy, based on "massive retaliation," also incurred criticisms of a more technical kind. How would NATO deal with minor assaults, say a preemptive Soviet occupation of West Berlin? Could the United States actually be relied upon to use its nuclear arsenal in a limited conflict? It had, after all, not done so in Korea, even when the battle seemed most desperate. A strategy that involved abandoning most of West Germany made no sense, once the Germans had begun to contribute conventional forces to NATO. Massive retaliation was above all a U.S. strategy, depending on the might of the U.S. Strategic Air Command. Massive retaliation assumed that the USSR would permanently remain much inferior in nuclear weaponry, and that the United States would remain invulnerable to Soviet assaults.

Both assumptions proved mistaken. In 1953 the Soviet Union exploded its first hydrogen bomb; in 1957 the Soviets launched Sputnik and demonstrated thereby their preeminent position in the field of ballistic missiles. Nuclear warfare henceforth threatened to become an artillery duel of global dimensions and inconceivable destructiveness. Such duels could not be tested in maneuvers; their strategy could not be derived from previous military history. They became the preserve of a new generation of civilian analysts who used war games as a substitute for real conflict.

Above all, NATO consistently underestimated its capacity for conventional defense, an easy mistake to make, especially at a time when the People's Republic of China was still allied to the Soviet Union. According to a widespread orthodoxy, the defense of Western Europe during the 1950s depended on nothing but the deterrent effect of the U.S. strategic air force. In assessing Soviet strength on land, however, Western experts may have overestimated the difficulties that the Soviets would have faced in suddenly concentrating huge forces for a surprise assault, or the problems of maneuvering huge mechanized forces through highly built-up areas on a narrow front. Westerners also were apt to overrate the value of non-Soviet divisions within the Warsaw Pact, many of which would have proved highly unreliable in the event of a conflict. Hence, as William Park, a British student of strategy, put it, "NATO was born with an inferiority complex regarding its conventional force capabilities, unwarranted even in the early years."[5]

On the U.S. side, the sense of inferiority went with the widespread conviction that the NATO allies somehow were unwilling to pull their weight. Both assumptions were open to serious doubt.* By

*By 1958, the European members' defensive expenditure as a percentage of their gross domestic product ranged from 7 for Britain, 6.8 for France, 4.7 for the Netherlands, 3.7 for Belgium, 3 for West Germany, and 2.9 for Denmark.

1958, the NATO powers had twenty-three divisions available for service in Western Europe, with another eighteen in Italy, as well as substantial forces in Southeastern Europe (twenty-two in Turkey, twelve in Greece). These could be reinforced by substantial reserves. These forces varied in composition and quality, but would surely have given a good account of themselves in a defensive campaign.

Neither was it true that the Europeans failed to pull their weight. By 1952–53, the United Kingdom and France were each spending an estimated 10 percent or more of their respective gross national product on defense. By 1953, the NATO Council was able to report that defense expenditure by NATO countries as a whole was 3.5 times higher than it had been in 1949. NATO forces were further strengthened from 1953 onward by a great array of tactical nuclear weapons. By the end of the 1950s, forward defense along West Germany's eastern border had ceased to be a chimera. No one of course can be sure what would have been the outcome of a war that was never fought. Nevertheless, Western Europe, by the end of the 1950s, was a great deal safer from Soviet attack than the policymakers imagined. In retrospect, General Lyman L. Lemnitzer (Supreme Allied Commander Europe, 1964–69) had good reason for his confident assertion that during the three decades that followed NATO's creation there was more stability in Europe than that continent had experienced in over a century.

Nonetheless, NATO's critics have been legion. They number within their ranks right-wingers, left-wingers, neutralists, isolationists, pacifists secular and pacifists religious, even though NATO members joined the alliance voluntarily, and remained of their own free will. The alliance would have astonished its founders by its longevity. Military cooperation facilitated economic and political collaboration. War-battered Europe regained confidence. The links between North America and Western Europe tightened rather than weakened. No transnational endeavor in the past achieved greater success. But the U.S. position was, and remains, quite different. There was no "overstretch" in arms expenditure. NATO therefore seems to this writer to have been one of the soundest political and military investments ever made, even though George Kennan and, earlier, President Kennedy had advised that the United States should do less in Europe and let the Europeans do more.

Part II

NATO:
From Defense
to Deterrence

France had joined NATO in part for reassurance against the Soviet Union, and even more so for the sake of preventing a future German *revanche* by locking West Germany into a common security system. Italy had welcomed integration into the Marshall Plan and NATO as a means of recovering its lost legitimacy and its former status as a major power. Italy in particular benefited from U.S. fears that it might fall prey to communism, from the strength of the Italian lobby in the United States, and from the tight links existing between Catholics in the United States and Catholics in Italy. In the post-Korean arms race, Italy obtained an end to the restrictions put on her by the postwar peace treaty. "There can be no doubt that Italy was a major beneficiary of the Cold War."[6] The Low Countries and Norway, for their part, remembered how neutrality before World War II had failed to serve their respective interests; all had endured the trauma of occupation; all were resolved to prevent such a disaster in future. Every NATO partner thus had a firm interest in making the alliance last.

To coordinate NATO was, nevertheless, a matter of considerable complexity. Though equal in theory, the partners were unequal in practice. The United States provided the leadership after 1950, a substantial body of troops, weapons for the rearmament of Germany, the greater part of the naval and air forces, and the bulk of the nuclear weaponry available to the Western allies. (The British and

French built their own nuclear deterrents, but these did not provide their respective owners with true strategic independence.)

NATO was, above all, more than a military alliance. It developed an extensive system of committees dealing with subjects as varied as political collaboration; the settlement of intra-alliance disputes; consultation on foreign policy; economic, scientific, technical, social, and cultural cooperation. The Secretary-General of NATO, who headed its international staff, became almost as powerful a man as the SACEUR. The alliance united policymakers and executives of many different nationalities in a common task. No other alliance in history had comprised such a diversity of partners or cooperated on such a broad range of subjects, nor lasted as long. (By the early 1980s, NATO comprised Belgium, Canada, Denmark, France, Greece, Iceland, Italy, Luxembourg, the Netherlands, Norway, Portugal, Spain, Turkey, the United Kingdom, the United States, and West Germany— enlarged in 1990 by the unification with East Germany, though with a special status within NATO.) No doubt NATO had its troubles, but these were kept in bounds and NATO worked. Contrary to all previous predictions and previous precedents, German, French, British, Dutch, Italian, and American military men cooperated successfully. NATO was an alliance whose members had joined freely; they were not simply satellites such as the Soviet Union's Warsaw Pact partners.

NATO's sense of inferiority vis-à-vis the Red Army was hardly justified. By the late 1950s, after West Germany had put in place a substantial new force, the *Bundeswehr*, the Western allies were already in fairly good shape, despite the Soviet Union's numerical superiority. The NATO forces moreover kept experimenting to improve their fighting capability. Overall, the NATO troops were better equipped and better trained. They had stronger logistic support and a better backup structure. NATO aircraft maintained on the average much higher sortie rates than their Warsaw Pact opponents. The Western allies were superior at sea. They enjoyed the advantage of interior defensive lines. Nobody of course knows how the alliance would have worked in the event of a Soviet attack. (The traffic problems that would have arisen from the clash of huge mechanized armies in the great conurbations of Western Europe would, alone, have been logistical nightmares—not to speak of the chaos that would have arisen from the employment of "tac-nukes.") But given the overcentralization and inflexibility of the Soviet forces, their morale problems, and the unreliability of the Soviets' Warsaw Pact allies, NATO would certainly have given a good account of itself.

The Debate over Nuclear Weapons

Even more contentious was the proposed use of nuclear weapons both on the tactical and the strategic level. It was NATO's sense of numerical inferiority which had first impelled the Europeans in NATO to demand that the United States defend them with tactical nuclear arms. (Eisenhower supported this policy which was, however, opposed by active-duty generals such as James Gavin, one of the outstanding U.S. airborne commanders of World War II.) The reason for the numerical balance was in the main budgetary. None of the Western allies were willing to match the Warsaw Pact armies in terms of manpower, tanks, and guns; the Europeans proposed and spent more money on social welfare than on the military, as Melvyn Krauss showed conclusively in his book, *How NATO Weakens the West.*[7] Initially NATO relied on its superiority in atomic weapons and on the qualitative superiority of its equipment. But these advantages evaporated as the Soviets improved their own armaments. During the 1950s, therefore, NATO began to deploy a great array of tactical nuclear weapons for direct battlefield support. (The French and British built their own nuclear deterrents—not so much to intimidate the Soviets as to assert French and British power within the Western councils. Existing treaty obligations forbade the Germans to do likewise.)

Of all the major Western powers, West Germany relied most heavily on the U.S. nuclear guarantee, and housed the largest number of battlefield nuclear projectiles on its soil. This dependency created its own psychological problems and its own peculiar ambivalence. The Germans wanted the United States to deploy tactical nuclear weapons on German soil so as to provide the maximum deterrent; the Germans looked to a "forward" defense entailing an allied stand on the Elbe River rather than on the Rhine. But at the same time German opinion—particularly left-wing opinion—dreaded the enormous concentration of atomic weapons on German soil that could turn Germany into a nuclear battlefield, and thereby spell *finis Germaniae,* an end to Germany.

Nuclear weapons, of course, could not be tested in maneuvers. In combat they would have turned any battlefield into a desert. By about 1957, NATO had deployed almost 7,000 tactical nuclear weapons in Europe. They included land mines, mortar rounds, recoilless rifle charges, air-dropped bombs, and artillery shells. Later, intermediate-range nuclear force missiles were added—at the Europeans' request, but nevertheless against bitter anti-U.S. opposition, especially from German, British, and Dutch pacifists and ecologists. Initially, the allies relied on a doctrine of massive retaliation, proclaimed by the United States in 1954, and officially adopted by NATO in 1957. Any Soviet assault would be met with the full might of the U.S. nuclear arsenal. The Soviets, however, themselves built a powerful nuclear rocket force. Allied superiority vanished, as the allies would not use their economic predominance to outbuild the Soviets at every step. In 1967 the NAC approved the Harmel Report on the Future Tasks of the alliance. The allies adopted a new doctrine of "flexible response," of measured retaliation. Missiles improved in quality and grew in quantity.

Equally contentious were the problems concerned with strategic nuclear weapons, that is to say intercontinental ballistic missiles. Initially, only the United States had the capacity to attack the Soviet

Union with nuclear bombs and destroy its main cities. As the Soviets improved their own weaponry, U.S. nuclear strategy was modified during the 1960s when Robert McNamara was secretary of defense. Deterrence of nuclear war rested on the country's assumed ability to absorb a nuclear strike and still destroy the Soviet Union. The Soviet Union, however, soon caught up to the United States. By the late 1960s, U.S. planners reconciled themselves to a doctrine aptly named MAD (for mutual assured destruction). According to prevailing orthodoxy at the time, any effort to upset this balance was destabilizing. As Stanley Kober, an arms expert, put it, "It was this logic that impelled McNamara passionately to oppose the construction of antiballistic missiles (ABMs)."[8] The United States thereafter tried to limit the construction of ABMs through accords such as the 1972 Strategic Arms Limitation Treaty (SALT I). But the Kremlin never accepted the U.S. strategic assumptions; the Soviets continued to work on ABM technology on the grounds that every weapon in history had always produced a counterweapon.

The MAD doctrine had far-reaching political consequences. The NATO allies all relied on the U.S. deterrent, yet they also had understandable doubts as to whether the Americans were truly willing to sacrifice New York for London, Paris, or Hamburg. Would the Soviets and Americans not be tempted to abstain from using strategic nuclear weapons, preserving their respective homelands as nuclear sanctuaries, while destroying both Western and Eastern Europe with tactical nuclear weapons? Fortunately, the world never found out. One thing is clear, however; until the 1980s the United States never attempted to use to the full its technical and scientific superiority in a race decisively to outarm the Soviet Union. (In building intercontinental ballistic missiles [ICBMs], the United States did not even aim at parity with the Soviet Union.) In our opinion, the failure of the United States to use to the full its capability was a grave mistake—not rectified until Ronald Reagan assumed the presidency (1981–88) and reordered U.S. priorities with massive rearmament.

Alone among the powers, the United States even set up an arms control lobby within its own bureaucracy, the Arms Control and Disarmament Agency (created in 1961). Dedicated to "balanced" arms reduction, the Agency formed a counterweight to the armed services. The Agency even maintained its own program to support doctoral dissertations, and thereby linked itself to a burgeoning arms-control lobby in academia. The arms controllers came to live in a world of their own, complete with a jargon quite incomprehensible to ordinary citizens. Intelligence proved even harder to obtain in closed societies such as East Germany (where the Soviets clandestinely set up intermediate-range ballistic missiles [SS-20s], detected only after the reunification of the East and West German armies). The Soviet Union was even harder to penetrate, for the Soviets falsified not merely statistics but even their cartography. They constructed, for example, an entire archipelago of secret cities (perhaps 100 in all). These were solely devoted to military research and arms production. These cities did not appear on any maps. Access to them was severely restricted; information on their work was unavailable.

United States arms controllers obviously remained much more ignorant. They had indeed access to reports submitted by spies and to evidence provided by satellites. But the former were of necessity scanty and contradictory, and the latter incomplete, because even the best images could provide little or no evidence of what went on inside the buildings photographed by satellites.

Quarrels over Burden-Sharing

In addition, there were constant quarrels within NATO concerning the allies' respective contribution to the alliance. Scholars such as Melvyn Krauss, especially, felt that the Europeans did not fully pull their weight and spent too much on welfare and not enough on defense. This assumption rested on comparative statistics for defense expenditure to which the United States always contributed the most as a percentage of the gross national product. Nevertheless, such comparisons could be misleading. The definition of defense spending included the costs of U.S. non-NATO defense commitments. Hence U.S. spending totals were biased by including the cost of maintaining U.S. forces in areas where the NATO allies had no treaty commitments. After all the United States saw itself as a global power with global responsibilities, especially to contain communism. NATO had regional responsibilities only. Comparisons concerning costs were apt also to take inadequate accounts of differentials; it was more expensive to maintain an American volunteer than a *Bundeswehr* conscript. (Within Western Europe itself, the NATO allies always supplied the bulk of the land forces— between 80 and 90 percent.)

Critics of NATO, year in and year out, kept saying that the United States bore the biggest burden, but actually the Europeans fielded more troops and spent a higher percentage of their GNP on NATO than did the United States until Reagan's presidency. Under General Alexander M. Haig, NATO Supreme Commander (1974–79), the members of the alliance all increased defense spending by a real 3 percent despite great economic hardships. NATO, during that period, decided to deploy theater nuclear weapons over Soviet threats and domestic pressure. Under Haig's command, NATO achieved greater readiness and enhanced coordination among its members.

Disputes about burden-sharing did not end the list of troubles that beset NATO. There were serious divisions both within the ranks of NATO's European partners, and between Europeans and Americans. Two allies—Greece and Turkey—almost came to blows over Cyprus. (Even long-standing allies such as Britain and France at times addressed one another in terms more suited to enemies than to allies.) Nevertheless, NATO worked. The ties between North America and Western Europe tightened; no trans-Atlantic endeavor in history achieved greater success. NATO worked effectively as both a military and a political alliance. In both capacities, NATO created a great array of new links between the United States and Western Europe. English became NATO's military lingua franca just as English became the standard language of air and sea communications. The United States furnished much of NATO's conventional, and most of its nuclear, weaponry; the United States supplied NATO's supreme commanders; the United States provided much of the advanced military technology and equipment. Many European officers and technicians were trained by Americans.

NATO also served as a channel for new ideas—sometimes with unintended consequences. NATO also influenced America. A great American army was stationed in Europe. Larger still was the number of American dependents, the wives and children of servicemen and civilian officials who, between them, created permanent American enclaves and intensified reciprocal relations between Western Europe and North America.

Was There a Real Soviet Threat?

In wider geo-strategic terms, NATO's full success will not become apparent until all military archives produced by the former Warsaw Pact states are open to inspection. However, a good deal of once-secret information has already been made available from the former German Democratic Republic. These records provide striking details concerning the aggressive nature of Warsaw Pact planning and, we should add, the mendacious character of Communist propaganda. Claiming to face an aggressive enemy, the Warsaw Pact leadership planned for massive offensives, supported by the first use of nuclear weapons. (In case of war, Warsaw Pact forces planned to strike through West Germany, Austria, Denmark, and thereafter occupy France.) Given the excellence of Soviet and East German intelligence services, the purely defensive nature of NATO's military planning was of course well known to the Warsaw Pact's leadership. This did not prevent Communist planners from consistently misrepresenting NATO's operational designs so as to conform to the aggressive image of the enemy created by Communist political warfare experts.

Despite its numerous and well-publicized deficiencies, NATO did deter the Soviet Union from blackmailing or "Finlandizing" the Western European countries. Deterrence worked because the United States remained faithful to its commitments. Without U.S. backing, the various continental states of Western Europe could hardly have stood up to Soviet pressure—particularly at a time when the Communist parties were powerful, especially in France and Italy. The Soviets, of course, tried to influence Western Europe through a variety of Communist fronts such as the World Federation of Trade Unions, and by propagandistic and diplomatic means. Except for a brief moment in 1974, however, when the existing Portuguese dictatorship toppled and the Portuguese Communist Party briefly hoped to gain power, Western Europe remained immune to Communist takeovers, or to being "Finlandized."

Diverted from Western Europe, the Soviet Union thereafter intensified its endeavors along what might be called the outer periphery of the Western world. By the early 1970s, the Vietnam War and the domestic unrest of the 1960s had weakened American self-confidence. Financial stability in the United States was threatened by inflation. By an act of deliberate abnegation, the United States had conceded to the Soviet Union an apparent superiority in missiles as well as in conventional arms. In addition, the Soviets, during the 1960s and 1970s, built a great navy, the world's second largest fleet. From Moscow's standpoint, Soviet military might would aid alike diplomacy, Soviet scholarship, and revolutionary expertise in promoting Third World "national wars of liberation"; these in turn would form stepping-stones on the road to worldwide victory for

Marxism-Leninism. Soviet propagandists in the West might laud "peaceful coexistence," but according to the official Marxist-Leninist theoreticians, it could only exist between rival state systems. There could be no peaceful coexistence between opposing social systems; conflict with capitalism was inevitable, and socialism Soviet-style was bound to win.

During the 1970s, the Soviets thus made substantial advances. Angola and Mozambique, formerly Portuguese colonies, emerged (1974) from colonial control as Marxist-Leninist republics, led by self-styled "vanguard parties." Indochina (South Vietnam, Cambodia, and Laos) and Ethiopia likewise fell under Marxist-Leninist governance, as did South Yemen. The Marxist-Leninist cause was sustained by a large Cuban expeditionary force (mainly deployed in Angola), by a direct Soviet invasion of Afghanistan (1979), and the establishment of a Marxist-Leninist government in Ethiopia and Nicaragua (with Cuban support). This huge effort looked impressive enough on the map—but none of the nations could be turned into effectively ruled dictatorships. On the contrary, armed oppositional groups continued to hold their own, massively supported by South Africa. The United States successfully backed anti-Soviet guerrillas in all the liberation-front states. Everywhere in the Third World, self-styled Marxist-Leninist movements met with defeats. Being limited in its operations to Western Europe, NATO had no direct part in this remarkable counterrevolution. The Soviet Union's main opponent throughout the world was the United States, but it effectively cooperated with individual NATO partners such as Britain and France, and NATO provided a secure center in Europe.

Contrary to Soviet predictions, the Marxist-Leninist tide thus proved neither irresistible nor irreversible. NATO held firm; so did its individual components. Instead it was the Soviet empire that began to falter—exhausted by the immense effort involved in holding and both exploiting and subsidizing its Eastern European dependencies, maintaining military primacy on the European continent, securing a naval presence on every ocean, and sustaining revolutionary commitment in the Third World.

In the long run the NATO allies were also surprisingly successful in keeping the military out of politics. West Germany's ability in creating the *Bundeswehr*, an army wholly loyal to the constitution, was one of the West's great success stories. The French army submitted to the Fourth Republic. The Spanish, Greek, and Portuguese armies, all heavily involved in politics, ultimately conformed to the constitutional pattern. At the same time the military gained or regained public trust. (In German as well as Russian and U.S. public opinion polls, the military remained the public institution in which respondents had the greatest degree of confidence.)

Partnership of Unequal Partners

NATO has not been without its problems. The alliance has been a partnership of unequal partners. The United States has contributed far more resources, both in absolute and relative terms, than did its allies. The United States controlled the bulk of NATO's nuclear weapons. Often there have been severe tensions between the United States and its European allies. (In 1966, for example, France withdrew from NATO's military command as a result of General de Gaulle's disagreements with Washington.) There have been dissensions between the European countries. (From 1974 until 1980 Greece pulled out of NATO's military affairs because of the Turkish invasion of Cyprus.) There have been clashes of opinion within the respective ruling establishments of each individual ally. (For instance, the French Ministry of Defense remained "Atlanticist" in orientation even during the height of de Gaulle's Franco-centric policies.)

These varying disputes have been expressed in many ways, even in shifts of military strategy. At a time when the United States held a massive superiority in nuclear weapons, NATO stood committed to the doctrine of "massive retaliation." Soviet advances in nuclear armaments, combined with intra-alliance politics, brought about a change in strategy toward the idea of "flexible response," officially enunciated in 1967; U.S. leadership within the alliance came under increasing criticism during the latter part of the Vietnam War when the United States withdrew many of its best officers and NCO's from Europe, and when its military morale strikingly declined. In 1969 a "Euro-Group" was established within NATO itself to facilitate co-operation with NATO's European partners.

Other disagreements within NATO and the EEC hinged on wider questions of policy toward the Soviet Union, as Europeans and Americans accused one another of being capricious or unreliable in their respective allegiances. For example, when the Berlin Wall was built in 1961, President Kennedy disappointed the West Germans by doing too little. The ranks of the disillusioned included Willy Brandt, then lord mayor of West Berlin, who thereafter became converted to a conciliatory *Ostpolitik*, which in turn offended the United States. Throughout the 1970s, Bonn pursued a policy of détente (cooperation with the Soviet Union), but then again it was Chancellor Helmut Schmidt of West Germany who in 1977 put pressure on the United States to defend Western Europe adequately, and to respond to the buildup of Soviet SS-20 missiles that could reach all of Europe. Such quarrels continued, as Western Europeans and Americans alike remained ambivalent about the unequal relationship, which compelled Europeans to rely on a U.S. nuclear "umbrella" while the Europeans supplied all the bases and the bulk of NATO's conventional manpower.

Despite all these quarrels, NATO's achievements remain remarkable. NATO had built a formidable army, for forward defense. By 1988, the NATO forces amounted to a million men in North and

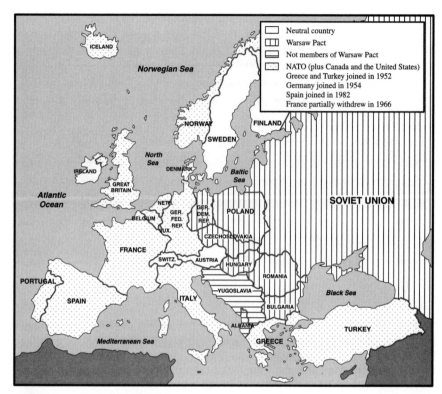

MAP 1   Europe in the Cold War

Central Europe, and another million in Southern Europe. The combat formations in North and Central Europe, the most exposed sector of NATO, in 1989, stood at eighteen armored divisions, twenty-three mechanized divisions, and six infantry and airborne divisions. Given the existing weaknesses in the Warsaw Pact armies, and given especially the unreliability of the Soviet allies within the pact, NATO's strength facilitated further European integration and helped restore legitimacy to Germany and Italy, the defeated powers, and reconciled Germany's neighbors, especially France, to a rearmed and economically dominant Germany. It was NATO that allowed domestic institutions to return to Germany and Italy.

Constitutional government and multi-party democracy flourished thanks to the peace, prosperity, and security created by NATO.

Although the United States had not approved of Europe's détente policy, President Nixon adopted it. Détente with the Soviet Union continued through the Carter administration until Reagan became president. He restored U.S. power and prestige internationally by increasing defense expenditure, by deploying Intermediate Nuclear Forces (INF) in Europe, and by telling the Soviet Union that détente was over. During President Carter's period of "disarmed diplomacy," Carter had refused to deploy short-range missiles in Europe. But the key to victory in the Cold War was the placing of intermediate missiles in Western Europe, and then the Strategic Defense Initiative. Soviet leader Gorbachev realized he couldn't win the Cold War and in 1989 he, in effect, gave up. NATO, under U.S. leadership, had won the Cold War. Without NATO and the United States, the Russians would have been able to Finlandize Europe. NATO's critics, such as Melvyn Krauss, were proven wrong; a nuclear-disarmed NATO without U.S. forces could not have won the Cold War, or remained independent of the Soviet Union. Once the INF had been deployed, Reagan could negotiate from strength. He got the Soviets back to the negotiating table and was conciliatory. He could afford to be, because the United States had rearmed and the Soviets could not keep up the arms race.

National Components

NATO operated as a transnational organization with a complex, indeed an overly complex, structure. But in the last instance, the alliance depended for its effectiveness on the strength of its individual national components. Armies by their very nature are among the most "national" of all institutions, and reflect alike the weakness and the strength of their respective nation states. Armies moreover are apt to intervene in politics during major national crises when civilian authority has lost credibility. Several European armies did interfere, make the attempt, or were suspected of disloyalty. In every case civilian rule prevailed; armies returned to the barracks. At the same time their technical efficiency and sophistication clearly increased. Relatively backward countries on Western Europe's rural periphery—Turkey, Greece, Spain, Portugal—continued to rely on relatively large conscript armies. As industrialization proceeded, the general trend was toward smaller forces with a growing percentage of highly trained regulars and soldiers on extended contracts (*Zeitsoldaten*, in *Bundeswehr* parlance). It was in France, as well as the aforesaid southern countries, that armies intervened, or had earlier intervened, in politics. But in the end neither Greek colonels nor Spanish generals prevailed in politics.

Most problematical of all was the French army. It had suffered a shattering defeat at German hands in 1940—but many more troubles would follow. The army was rebuilt, an uneasy amalgamation of Free French troops loyal to de Gaulle from the beginning, colonial forces that rallied to the general after the allied invasion of North Africa, elements of the French regular army, and partisans, mostly Communists, organized into the "French Forces of the Interior." This army gave a good account of itself at the end of World War II, but nevertheless suffered from a collective sense of inferiority. The French army depended at first almost entirely on foreign (mainly U.S.) equipment; the soldiers looked ragged and unfamiliar in their U.S.- and British-made uniforms; the officers were poor men within the world's military profession, for the planners of the Fourth Republic had little interest in military matters, and thought above all of modernizing the French economy. True enough, the French army secured some excellent officers; Frenchmen bore the burden of conscription without much complaint. Morale was shattered by two successive defeats: The French lost the colonial war in Indochina (1945–54). Then came the Algerian debacle (1945–62), a traumatic event that led to de Gaulle's accession to the presidency and the formation of the Fifth Republic.

De Gaulle reformed the armed forces, just as he reformed the constitution. Not that the army lived up to its reputation of *la grande muette* (the great silent one); *la grande bavarde* (the great talker) would have been a more suitable description. But de Gaulle did rid the army of the rightists, as earlier he got rid of Communists. The army's loyalty to the Republic was assured; never again would dashing *paras* or dour Foreign Legionaries attempt to challenge civilian authority. The army remained a fairly popular institution; France never developed a peace movement comparable in scale and intensity to Holland's, Britain's, or West Germany's. (Overall the peace movements and the protests against nuclear arms were more powerful in Protestant than in Catholic countries.) At the same time de Gaulle modernized the armed forces. De Gaulle was determined to end the Algerian War, in part because he wished to transform an army composed mainly of infantry, deployed in Algeria, to an army strong in armor, backed by nuclear weapons, an army fit to regain for France her accustomed position as a great military power. In large measure he succeeded. The quality of French armaments vastly increased; France developed into a nuclear power; the army became highly mobile (with eight armored divisions, two mechanized infantry divisions, three partly mechanized infantry divisions, and a parachute division by 1979). France acquired a leading position in certain military industries. (By 1991, for example, France occupied the first place in the world for military software.) Though not formally part of NATO's military command, these forces could not have avoided involvement, had the Soviets ever launched an attack against Western Europe. Concluded a U.S. military expert, "with capabilities extending across the full range from a militia to a nuclear force, France possesses a flexibility of military options unmatched by any other Western European nation."[9]

West Germany

Even more surprising was the success attained by the German *Bundeswehr*, under what appeared unfavorable circumstances at the time. When World War II ended, the Allies were determined to wipe out German military power for all time. "Reeducation" in postwar Germany in fact worked—though not in the sense anticipated by U.S. advocates of reeducation. World War II left Germans disillusioned with the military. German rearmament under Konrad Adenauer occurred, not in response to German popular agitation, but mainly in response to allied demands for a West German contribution to Western military defense after a series of major crises—the Berlin blockade in 1948, the detonation of the first Soviet atom bomb in 1949, the North Korean attack on South Korea in 1950, and the development of a military force in East Germany (the *Kasernierte Volkspolizei*, started in 1952, renamed *Nationale Volksarmee* in 1956).

When recruiting began for the *Bundeswehr*, the new army met with widespread opposition. Liberal and left-wing critics (especially the Social Democrats) feared that the army would become a school of militarism and a danger to West Germany's democratic institutions. The hard-line right, by contrast, was contemptuous of the new army on the grounds that it was soft, that the *Bundeswehr's* new doctrine of *"Innere Führung"* (discipline through self-discipline) would never work. The *Bundeswehr*, the charge sheet continued, was not a genuinely German institution, but an instrument of allied policy, more highly integrated into NATO than any other of its components, and lacking even its own General Staff. The *Bundeswehr* also faced far-reaching political and moral problems of a kind that sprang from Germany's troubled past. Should the *Bundeswehr* attempt to take over any military traditions derived from the Nazi *Wehrmacht* or the Imperial German Army? Was there, or was there not, a "usable past" for a democratic German army? Could a German soldier be expected to fight in a future conflict that would certainly pit *Bundeswehr* against the *Nationale Volksarmee*—Germans against Germans? None of Germany's allies confronted such moral predicaments.

Nevertheless the *Bundeswehr* turned out to be one of West Germany's most outstanding achievements, paralleling in the military sphere West Germany's success in building an effective political democracy, and the strongest economy on European soil. From being treated with suspicion by a considerable segment of West Germany's population, the army gained popular acceptance. In words ascribed to Hitler, the Third Reich had relied on a Royal Prussian Army, an Imperial Germany Navy, and a National Socialist *Luftwaffe*. The new *Bundeswehr*, by contrast, was loyal to the democratic order. (To the surprise of antimilitarists, officers and enlisted men within the *Bundeswehr* were actually more sympathetic toward organized resistance against the Hitler regime, and also to the role of opposition parties, than was the population at large.) The *Bundeswehr's* officer corps continued to contain a substantial number of noblemen, and also sons of former officers and civil servants. The West German officer corps, however, was nowhere near as inward-looking as the French officer corps (with a large component of officers who were themselves sons of officers and noncommissioned officers). But there was none of the class sentiment that had characterized the *Reichswehr* (the army of the Weimar Republic) as much as the Imperial German Army.

Britain

The British armed forces likewise occupied a key position in Western defense, though their composition strikingly changed. Before World War II the Royal Navy had been the world's first, Britain's "Senior Service." As British imperial power declined worldwide, Britain's navy dropped to third place in terms of manpower deployed by the three

British services. (The Royal Air Force came second, the army first.) Global strategy altered as the Suez Canal lost in importance, and the Cape route gained accordingly. (By the early 1960s supertankers of over 100,000 tons were in operation; these could not be accommodated even after the Canal had been widened.) Another break came with the Harold Wilson government's decision to withdraw all British forces from east of Suez (1967–68). The navy became primarily a small-ship fleet fit above all for antisubmarine warfare. Even so, the Royal Navy continued as the mainstay of NATO's European naval forces. The British likewise built their own nuclear deterrent—mainly developed like its French equivalent—for the purpose of legitimating its owner in the desired status of a great power.

Henceforth Britain's main defensive role was on land, as it had been in the days of Henry V in the fifteenth century. During the immediate postwar period, the British army was particularly important; Britain at first supplied the bulk of the soldiers available to the Western allies in Europe. The British continued conscription, but in 1957, after the Suez debacle, they reverted once more to an all-professional force. The new regular army was highly efficient, and much better paid than the prewar professional army. Recruits came from the ranks of skilled workers and technicians—not from the farm laborers and urban laborers who had once volunteered for Queen Victoria's army. The officer corps still retained some of the old class structure (with a substantial intake of public-school boys and now also many graduates from Catholic boarding schools). But relations between officers and men were much easier than in the old conscript army; the road to promotion lay open to all qualified men.

The new army spent less time on the parade ground than the old conscript army, less time with the regimental barber; it was highly proficient in a technical sense. The Green Jackets (light infantry), cavalry, and Guards regiments, known as the "Black Mafia," tended to get most of the best jobs; they looked down on the infantry, who in turn looked down on the noncombatants. But overall it was a remarkable body, one of the most successful institutions in postwar Britain. It was a model of a democratic force whose loyalty to the civilian government was never questioned. It also displayed great operational efficiency.

The British army maintained a substantial commitment to NATO. (Between three and four divisions were deployed in Germany.) The army also became involved once more in the never-ending disputes of Northern Ireland. In 1969 almost an entire division departed to Northern Ireland where Catholics clashed with local security forces dominated by Protestants. Initially, most Catholics welcomed the British imperial troops, but the honeymoon soon ended, and the British found themselves equally disliked by both parties—but at least full-scale civil war was avoided. The army also remained capable of fighting a conventional war thousands of miles away from its home base—as the Argentinians found out in the Falkland War of 1982.

The British, like American intellectuals, were apt to shy away from triumphalism and nationalist conceit. In fact the British army performed outstandingly well. It was also alone among Western armies in winning every post–World War II guerrilla campaign in the Third World—against the Mau Mau rebels in Kenya, the Chinese Communists in Malaya, and the Indonesians in North Borneo.

The United States

It was, however, the U.S. military that provided NATO's sheet anchor. The U.S. military was unique; it was the only Western force with a worldwide commitment; it provided the world's largest navy, the main part of Western nuclear weaponry, the greatest air force, and a substantial land force. Without the presence of the Seventh Army in Southern Germany, Western Europe's defense would have lacked credibility. When the war ended the U.S. Army had been Europe's second largest. But, as after every great conflict in U.S. history, the Americans rapidly permitted their army to decline in number and quality. By the time of the Berlin blockade, the U.S. Army could field only a single division and a few additional regiments in

Germany—this at a time when Soviet propaganda was at its height in accusing Washington of planning aggression. Following North Korea's invasion of South Korea, the Americans, however, rapidly increased their forces in NATO from 1950 on (to a total of five divisions by the 1960s), with a powerful tactical air force as a complement to the army's armored counterattack capability.

The U.S. military met with a variety of woes that mirrored those of U.S. society at large. The military suffered from interservice rivalry among army, air force, navy, and marines. There was overlapping of functions, and duplication of services (especially with regard to logistics and maintenance). The U.S. military was highly bureaucratized—more so even than, say, the British defense establishment. Military, like civilian, society displayed the characteristic U.S. admiration for gadgetry, politicking, endless experimentation, and the self-proclaimed expertise of civilian consultants. More than any other, the U.S. military was influenced by industrial and engineering models, with an emphasis on cramming facts.

These weaknesses were multiplied by the Vietnam War. As pointed out before, the selective draft worked in an inequitable fashion; there was bitter political opposition. The Seventh Army in West Germany was depleted of its best officers and noncommissioned officers. Morale slumped; drunkenness and drug addiction became common; there was pervasive disrespect for authority, and also mounting crime and racial friction. At the same time inflation reduced the soldier's real pay; to foreigners, especially Germans, the U.S. Army suddenly appeared a host of drunken paupers, and the U.S. Army's prestige slumped accordingly.

Fortunately, the U.S. military's weaknesses were balanced by great strengths. The U.S. Armed Forces possessed an enormous capacity for rapid improvisation and for recuperation from disaster. In World War II an army composed mainly of civilians in uniform had learned from its mistakes, and defeated the professional *Wehrmacht* and the equally professional Japanese Imperial forces. The Americans had successfully defended South Korea against North Koreans and Chinese. In Viet-nam the Americans had defeated the Viet Cong and North Vietnamese Communist forces in every major engagement. The Americans had been defeated politically, however; their military status would thereafter be raised by political means. President Nixon ended the draft (a process completed in 1973), but the effects were ambivalent at best.

The professionalization of the military created a psychological rift between professional middle-class people (who rarely served) and the military. The all-volunteer military opened many new op-portunities to black Americans. (Together with athletics the military had the best record in successfully integrating men of all races.) On demobilization, veterans of any color moreover transferred technical training, discipline, and self-confidence into productive civilian careers. The professional army thereby acted as an instru-ment for social advancement. (Contrary to a widespread miscon-ception, the U.S. Army was never at any time an underclass army.)

Overall, however, the "all-volunteer force" regained its former efficiency. Re-equipment began in the late 1970s, and was com-pleted during the Reagan presidency, which vastly added to the army's fighting capacity. In a more general sense, the military in later years increasingly came to be commanded by men who had served as combat officers in Vietnam, men conversant with high-tech weaponry, determined to avoid past military mistakes, and reluctant also to fight abroad without solid political support at home. From the late 1960s onward, the military created an integrated force in which poor people of any race could gain advancement. "For poor blacks and poor whites there simply was nothing like the army. . . . The ap-pointment in 1977 of Clifford Alexander, a black, as the Secretary for the Army seemed to ratify what was occurring at all levels."[10]

In a wider sense, it was the U.S. military that played the decisive part in keeping NATO together. Senior officers proved adroit politi-cians, employing skills honed at home with much credit abroad. Of-ficers persuaded their allies to cooperate in joint maneuvers, joint weapons projects, joint diplomatic initiatives. Having learned to co-operate effectively with the British in World War II, they now mastered the art of joint decisionmaking on innumerable subcommittees and committees, commissions, and headquarters groups. Without this cement, NATO might easily have broken asunder.

There were also striking changes in weaponry as the high-tech revolution changed military procurement. By the late 1970s, the threat of massive nuclear exchanges between the superpowers had lost credibility, while the Soviets continued to outweigh NATO strength in conventional forces. But the NATO powers continued to outdo the Soviet Union and its allies in high-tech, applied to the military through improvements in fields such as ECM (electronic countermeasures) and a series of technical innovations, collectively known as "Stealth," the name of a new bomber invisible to Soviet radar. Military reform had started under President Carter only in 1978 after a period of "disarmed diplomacy." It was much extended during the Reagan presidency, and applied by the United States on the battlefield under President Bush. As Harold Brown, Carter's former defense secretary put it, "We designed the high-tech weapons, the Reagan administration bought 'em and trained people to use 'em, and the Bush administration used 'em [in the Gulf War]."

Weapons on their own, of course, do not decide wars. The United States also improved in general war-fighting capability (for instance, by developing the concept of an "air-land battle" entailing deep penetration of the enemy's rear echelons) so as to shatter massive formations poised for assault. The Soviets apparently became convinced that they could not possibly win a land war in Western Europe. The Gulf War subsequently provided a devastating demonstration of U.S. military superiority.

As the Cold War ended, the extent of NATO's success was all too easily overlooked. According to many Cold War theoreticians, including even former Secretary of Defense James Schlesinger, the bipolar world of the Cold War had imposed on the two superpowers a unique system of restraint insofar as each side recognized the constraints implicit in each other's capacity for massive retaliation. Supposedly there was an unintended order in this bipolar system, a global equilibrium, ultimately thrown into disarray by the dissolution of the Soviet empire. Unfortunately this analysis obscures reality. As Jonathan Clark, a U.S. foreign policy expert, eloquently put it:

> . . . the facts cannot be forgotten so readily. The Soviet Union really did try to blockade Berlin and draw Greece behind the Iron Curtain; children really did hide under their desks during the Cuban missile crisis; Soviet tanks really did roll into Prague, Budapest, and Kabul; on Soviet orders, refugees really were shot and allowed to bleed to death under the Berlin Wall; dictatorships in Cuba, Ethiopia, Angola, and Mozambique really did rise on the backs of Soviet-equipped and -trained security services; state sponsors to anti-American terrorism really were fêted in Moscow; the Soviet Union really did bankroll the Communist parties of Western Europe and Latin America. None of this was a dream. To combat all this, the West really did live on the nuclear high wire. And as for conventional war during the Cold War, the history books burgeon with the records of major conflagrations.[11]

These were indeed dangerous years for the West. For all its errors, NATO played an essential part in reducing their perils. The world had much for which to be grateful.

Part III

NATO: From Defense to Détente

From its beginnings, NATO faced numerous troubles. Each of the allies had its own separate national interests, and its own military culture.[12] NATO's intelligence was deficient. The U.S. spy-masters, in particular, gravely underestimated the proportion of the Soviet Union's gross national product devoted to armaments, while overestimating the Soviet Union's economic production. Western intelligence officers had excessively high regard for the morale and striking capability of the Warsaw Pact force, but they failed to understand the extent of ethnic rivalries within the Soviet Union, and of the social disintegration at work within it. "That, too, was an intelligence failure of major proportions."[13] There were numerous shifts in strategy, both conventional and nuclear. Planning for conventional war veered from a cautious strategy of initial retreat to "forward defense" (to please the Germans). Nuclear strategy turned from initial designs for "massive retaliation" to graduated response.[14] But in the final analysis, no expert had any realistic idea of how a conventional war could be stopped from spilling into a nuclear encounter, and how a nuclear war itself could be fought successfully. Weapons proved hard to standardize, intelligence difficult to coordinate. There were all manner of disagreements on how the alliance should be led. Nevertheless, NATO stayed together, deterred the Soviets, and integrated Germany into a collective defense system for the West.

Defense, Victory, and Reorganization

In terms of population and economic production, the NATO powers greatly outnumbered the Warsaw Pact states. For financial reasons, however, the NATO powers were never prepared to translate this superiority into military terms. The combined Warsaw Pact armies were thus considerably stronger than the NATO forces. In consequence, the NATO states were under persistent pressure to keep modernizing their forces to maintain a qualitative superiority. This was not an easy task, especially as the cost of equipment continued to rise, reflecting the ever-increasing complexity of modern weapons. Advanced armaments in turn required highly trained, hence expensive, personnel. Any soldier had been able to handle the M1 rifle of World War II; a modern infantryman, by contrast, had to be a highly trained specialist.

Above all, NATO had to cope with the perils of prosperity. Growing wealth diminished the lure of military life. So did the European peace movements, particularly popular among the young and the academically educated (especially in Germany, a country once renowned for its militarism.) Declining birthrates lessened the number of eligible recruits; so did the growing popularity of "alternate civilian service," available to German and French conscripts in particular. In effect, the task of modernizing or rebuilding the armed forces fell, above all, on the officers of field rank, as a group the most flexible and most innovative men within the armed forces.

NATO was further troubled by continuous disputes over burden-sharing.[15] These reflected striking disparities between the relative military expenditure of the various partners as a percentage of their gross domestic product, as indicated by the accompanying table referring to the position in 1991.

Country	Percentage of GDP
United States	5.6
Britain	3.9
France	3.6
Germany	2.8
Italy	2.1
Canada	2.00
Spain	1.8

SOURCE: *The Economist*, London, Dec. 25, 1993 to Jan. 7, 1994.

Why should rich Germans spend a much lesser proportion of their resources on the common defense than British, not to speak of U.S. citizens? In their defense, Europeans such as Helmut Schmidt argued that statisticians underrepresented the value of the European, including the German, contribution. (In terms of manpower, the European contribution to NATO's standing forces in Europe was as follows: manpower 91 per cent, divisions 96 per cent, tanks 86 per cent, artillery pieces 95 per cent, combat aircraft 82 per cent, major fighting ships at sea in European waters and the Atlantic 70 per cent.[16]) The United States, admittedly, supplied the bulk of nuclear weapons. It is also true that U.S. military expenditure was bound to constitute a higher percentage of its GDP than was the case with any of its partners, because it had much larger global commitments than they did.

Existing arrangements gave to the United States many obvious and not so obvious advantages. The United States enjoyed undisputed primacy within the alliance—U.S. troops were kept in a high state of readiness. Membership in NATO provided some consistency to U.S. foreign policy at a time when the public and politicians kept vacillating between isolationism and interventionism.

Above all, NATO worked in both the civilian and the military sense. It was under the aegis of NATO that free institutions took root in Germany, Italy, Portugal, Greece, and Turkey. It was under NATO's auspices that old rivals—Britain, Germany, France, Italy, Turkey, Greece—cooperated in a military sense. NATO kept the peace. As Helmut Schmidt pointed out in the article previously cited, this achievement rested on five principles: First came deterrence. Whatever their intentions, the Soviets understood that a war of aggression would not be cost-effective. Second, the alliance maintained credibility. (The Cuban crisis was the first and last open nuclear confrontation). Third, the NATO leaders stuck to proportionality of means; there was not a touch of adventurism to NATO planning. Fourth, NATO proved capable of constantly reevaluating its performance. Overall, the NATO forces in central Europe surpassed their opponents in flexibility and adaptability. Fifth, the alliance maintained a rough balance of security for both sides, and it did so for more than forty years.

In 1991, the Cold War ended with the Communist defeat. The Warsaw Pact broke up (April 1) and eight months later Boris Yeltsin and Mikhail Gorbachev announced the forthcoming dissolution of the Soviet Union. The Soviet army was succeeded by the Russian army. The Soviet Union's KGB empire disintegrated, as the Russian successor service changed its name and possibly its methods. For the first time in its history, NATO found itself without an enemy.

Revisionist scholarship in the West considered that we all lost the Cold War. Revisionists meant that the Cold War had entailed an immense misuse of precious resources, and a coarsening of politics all over the West. Such arguments, however, overlook the enormous military strength that the Soviet Union had deployed. As late as 1991, by which time a number of major reductions had been made, the Soviet Union had in uniform a total of about 4,000,000 men, with another 9,000,000 in reserve. The Soviet Union's land forces were by far the largest in Europe; the Soviet navy ranked as the

world's second; the Soviet ballistic missile forces and strategic avia-
tion were formidable—between them they formed the most awe-
some aggregation of military forces ever assembled in peacetime.
Even the German *Wehrmacht* as deployed by the Third Reich before World War II looked puny by comparison.

The Gorbachev revolution after 1985 at first made no difference
in this respect. As Ambassador Richard F. Staar has pointed out, Soviet arms spending continued to rise—this at disastrous cost to the
Soviet civilian economy, the Soviet consumer, and ultimately, to
the Soviet system as a whole. (According to Sergei M. Rogov of the
USSR Institute of the United States and Canada, military expenditure was expected to go up from 26 per cent of the Soviet budget to
36 per cent in 1991.) The Soviets continued to deploy advanced ver-
sions of intercontinental ballistic missiles, but also silo-based and
mobile ones. (The United States had no weapons in those cate-
gories.) The Soviets reportedly worked on new Delta ballistic missile submarines. The START treaty, signed between the United
States and the Soviet Union in July 1991, also permitted the Soviets
to maintain a great array of defensive weapons against ballistic missiles, aircraft, and Cruise missiles.[17] Again, the United States had no
comparable counterforce. Given such massive armaments, given
also the difficulties in verifying compliance with treaty obligations,
caution was in order for the Western powers.

Would Moscow have ever used this force against Western Europe? The secret intentions of Soviet policymakers will only be un-
covered when the archives of the former Soviet Union become
available to researchers—perhaps not even then. The declared doctrines of the Soviet armed forces had stressed the importance of surprise, deception, and the strategic initiative. Theirs was not a
defensive doctrine; they believed in the merits of a sustained offensive. Would Moscow have confined its military interests to safe-
guarding the Warsaw Pact from aggression? According to the
Soviets' own statements, the answer to this question is "no." Soviet

theoreticians had elaborated a doctrine of "proletarian internationalism" whereby the working class of one country might legitimately
give support to revolutions in other countries. It was on these
grounds that the Soviets had sent arms to Cuba and Vietnam,
Cuban proxy forces had fought in Angola and Ethiopia, and Soviet
troops had intervened in Afghanistan.

Would Soviet troops have intervened in Western Europe, had
there been no NATO alliance? We cannot be sure. We do know,
however, that during the Portuguese revolution of 1974, the pro-
Moscow Portuguese Communist Party briefly hoped to seize power
in Lisbon, intending to install a Communist dictatorship on the
Eastern European model. Nothing in Soviet doctrine or Soviet experience would have prevented Soviet forces from supporting their
Communist comrades in Portugal—or for that matter in Italy or
France, which also had large Communist parties—without NATO's
preventive armaments. NATO, however, had built an impressive deterrent force designed to contain any Soviet advance, and to prevent
military blackmail at the conference table. In the end, NATO
won without firing a shot. NATO's bloodless victory was unique in
history—as complete as it was unforeseen. For all its weaknesses,
NATO effectively protected Western Europe—and at a reasonable
cost and without scrimping on social expenditure.

In 1989, during its last year, the Warsaw Pact powers, for the first
time, announced a defensive doctrine; they enunciated a somewhat
ill-defined doctrine of "reasonable sufficiency." Within two years,
the Soviet forces were preparing to withdraw from Eastern Europe,
thus completely altering the strategic balance. In 1992, the former
Soviet Union, by then reconstituted as the CIS (Commonwealth of
Independent States), agreed that the member-states would form
their own separate armies. The former Soviet armed forces would
therefore be divided. (Ukraine proceeded to form its own army im-
mediately.) Belarus, Ukraine, and Kazakhstan publicly announced
their intention of becoming nuclear-free states—but as Graham Al-

lison, an American expert, put it, "Do not count on today's preferences lasting as circumstances change or less responsible people become more influential."[18] The position as yet remained uncertain, with tensions between Russia and Ukraine over the future of the Black Sea fleet, Crimea, and nuclear weaponry remaining in Ukraine, as well as conflict continuing in several states in Central Asia and in Moldova and Georgia.

Imperial Breakup

Contrary to Marxist forecasts, it was the Soviet empire that broke, not NATO. The dissolution of the Soviet empire involved the most far-reaching act of decolonization experienced in modern history. Having unwisely preached decolonization abroad, the Soviet empire now suffered it at home. Post-Communist Russia (the Russian Federation) was smaller even than the rump state left by the Treaty of Brest Litovsk, imposed by victorious Germany on Russia in 1917. The Baltic states (Estonia, Latvia, Lithuania), Belarus, Ukraine, the southern Muslim states, most of the trans-Caucasus gone! Not surprisingly, the Russian armed forces had to cope with indiscipline, crime, poor living conditions, poor morale, and corruption. Overall performance deteriorated, as shown in the Russians' half-botched reconquest of Chechnya (1994–95), a dissident Muslim province of the Russian Caucasus. "The Great Patriotic War" (World War II) had helped to legitimize the Soviet regime half a century earlier; from the late 1980s, by contrast, wartime glory had tarnished in the eyes of successive generations. Instead, there was now a new gangsters' *internationale* which linked Russian syndicates with criminal organizations worldwide. Not surprisingly, experts feared that, in addition to conventional weapons, atomic, bacteriological, or chemical weapons might find their way into the arsenals of terrorists or of outlaw governments.

NATO therefore faced an entirely new set of challenges. NATO somewhat simplified its overly complex command structure.* The military forces in central Europe thinned out. The border zone between NATO and the Warsaw Pact had once been the most highly militarized region in history, with something like three million men on both sides of the frontier, and a huge accumulation both of conventional and nuclear weapons. (Even a conventional clash between the huge opposing armored and mechanized forces, each with enormous firepower, would have devastated the region, and produced an ecological as well as an economic and demographic catastrophe.) On November 19, 1990, by the time the Soviet empire was faltering, the NATO and Warsaw Pact members signed an unprecedented Treaty on Conventional Armed Forces in Europe (CFE). The treaty imposed equal ceilings on nonnuclear weapons located between the Atlantic Ocean and the Ural Mountains, limiting each side to 20,000 tanks, 20,000 artillery pieces, 30,000 armored combat vehicles, 6,000 combat aircraft, and 2,000 attack helicopters. The treaty also imposed restrictions on where these forces were to be deployed.

Although the CFE has been successful so far, in 1995 disagreements developed over the "flank zones." The treaty had put restrictions on forces in northwestern Russia and in the Northern Caucasus Military District in southwestern Russia. Because of unrest in Chechnya and other parts of the Caucasus, the Russians claimed they could not comply with force restrictions in Article V of the treaty. Failure of CFE would hurt European security and would damage Russian relations with its neighbors and the United States.

*As of July 1994, NATO's northern flank was placed under Allied forces North West Europe (AFNORTHWEST); NATO's southern flank was headed by Allied Forces Southern Europe (AFSOUTH). Ill-fated attempts at peacekeeping in Bosnia were entrusted to a United Nations Protection Force (UNPROFOR), composed mainly of NATO troops.

"It would adversely affect ratification of the START II arms control agreement by the Russian State Duma and U.S. Senate while delaying . . . economic assistance to the Russian Federation, including Nunn-Lugar funding."[19] Further arms control negotiations would also be harmed if CFE failed. The Organization for Security and Cooperation in Europe (OSCE) and many north and south-central European states and the Baltics would feel their security was at risk. This could lead them to demand immediate admission into NATO to protect themselves against a Russian threat.

Like all disarmament agreements, this accord proved hard to enforce. In 1995, moreover, the West agreed to extensive concessions in order to reduce tensions between NATO and Russia over the Chechnyan and Bosnian issues. (The West allowed Russia to deploy more weapons in the regions adjoining Europe than was permitted under the treaty, this at a time when the Russians needed massive troop concentrations to hold down Chechnya.) When all is said and done, however, both the West and Russia profited from the dispersal of the huge arms concentrations on both sides of the Elbe River. NATO forces in Europe strikingly diminished in numbers (from 3,151,800 men in 1985 to 2,753,600 men in 1992, with further reductions thereafter). In 1993, Russia and the United States signed an agreement known as START II (confirming a Joint Understanding between Presidents Bush and Yeltsin in 1992). The signatory powers pledged to make substantial reductions in their strategic warheads; they also promised to reduce their submarine-based missiles; they banned intercontinental ballistic missiles with multiple independently targeted reentry vehicles. The agreement reflected the striking improvement that had taken place in U.S.-Russian relations. But like so many other disarmament agreements, the accord depended on the mistaken assumption that the intelligence services of one country could clearly find out the details of another country's armory—the number of its warheads, of its rocket-launching sites, and their state of preparedness.* Above all, accords must rely on mutual confidence—which is hard to attain when partners rapidly change their minds for reasons of internal politics. (In 1995 Presidents Clinton and Yeltsin thus announced major plans for the exchange of nuclear data and weapons inspection. Less than a year later, the Russians essentially suspended the talks, Yeltsin having been forced to remove nearly all pro-Western reformers from his government.)

The classic doctrine of "forward defense" gave way to a new concept that relied on smaller, more flexible forces. The military adjusted to the information revolution in the civil sphere, and elaborated new techniques of remote-sensing, precision-guided weapons, and communications. Their development would center, above all, on the United States, now by far the biggest defense spender on the globe.** In Europe, battlefield nuclear weapons disappeared; medium-range nuclear weapons would stay in NATO arsenals, but no longer be constantly deployed on surface vessels and submarines. A much larger proportion of NATO forces than hitherto would consist of reserves. NATO likewise adopted a new crisis management strategy, a new Allied Command Europe (ACE). This entailed a cut by two-thirds of the U.S. forces in Europe, and the creation of a multinational Rapid Reaction Force (RRF, with its headquarters at Bielefeld, Germany). The new force would number

*The projected manpower reductions from 1992 to 1994 were as follows (in thousands): Belgium: 81–40. Canada: 84–76. Denmark: 29–25. France: 432–371. Germany: 447–300. Greece: 159–159. Italy: 354–287. Netherlands: 93–70. Norway: 33–25. Portugal: 58–no information. Spain: 217–170 or 190. Turkey: 560–360. United Kingdom: 293–241. U.S.: 1914–1355. For details see International Institute of Strategic Studies, *The Military Balance 1993–1994* (London, Brassey's, 1993), special diagram for command structure, p. 47, and comparative tables of defense expenditure and military manpower, p. 224.
**According to *The Economist*, July 10, 1995, "Survey of Technology," p. 7, defense spending (in billion dollars) stood as follows: U.S.: 297.6. Russia: 113.8. China: 56.2. France: 42.6. Japan: 41.7. Germany: 36.7. Britain: 34. Italy 20.6.

100,000 men. The RRF would be in a position to repel small attacks anywhere in Europe, and NATO thereby acquired new flexibility.

Under the new dispensation, East Germany became part of NATO through fusion with West Germany. At the height of their power, the East German armed forces had numbered 170,000 men, part of the Warsaw Pact's military elite, and the last German stronghold of Prussian military discipline. (Old-fashioned West Germans, anti-Communist to the core, used to watch with tears in their eyes the changing of the guard in East Berlin where such matters were still done properly.) Henceforth, the *Bundeswehr* took over about 10,000 East German professionals (all below the rank of colonel, and all obliged to enlist at ranks lower than their former position.) The *Bundeswehr* successfully integrated East Germans into the German army, and therefore played a major, though little regarded, role in German unification. (Just as the U.S. military had turned out to be the most successful of U.S. public institutions in integrating whites and blacks, the *Bundeswehr* proved the most effective of German institutions in joining "Ossies" and "Wessies.") At the same time the *Bundeswehr* diminished in size, to 370,000 men, with further cuts to follow. Germany therefore was left with a defense force smaller than that of France—the *beau idéal* of French military planners since the creation of the Bismarckian Reich (1870). At the same time, progress continued in the "internationalization" of NATO forces through the creation of mixed corps (including the two U.S.-German corps, a mixed German-French-Spanish corps, and a German-Dutch corps in process of formation).

Within the NATO alliance, the future role of the Western European Union (WEU) is of major importance to U.S. geo-political concerns. WEU originated in the Brussels Treaty concluded in 1948 between Britain, France, and the Benelux countries, and at the time Britain was by far the strongest power within this grouping. Its original object was to provide security against the resurgence of a vengeful and defeated Germany, as much as against Soviet ambitions. The

United States did not join WEU and promoted NATO instead. In 1954 the Brussels Treaty Organization and NATO admitted and rearmed West Germany, and the Brussels Treaty Organization was transformed into WEU. WEU has its own parliamentary assembly, and its own secretariat. All real work regarding defense was, however, done by NATO, and WEU's role in successive confrontations with the Soviet Union was limited.

It was only from the mid-1980s onward that WEU's members decided to reactivate the organization, part of Europe's search for a new political and military identity. (It now includes all EU states except Ireland, Greece, and Denmark.) In 1987 an agreement was reached on a "Platform of European Security Interests," and WEU thereafter sought to extend its membership in accordance with the Single European Act of 1986. WEU has become the "European pillar" of the transatlantic alliance for which President John F. Kennedy had once called with verve and prescience. WEU seems more suitable for this task than the Independent European Program Group (IEPG), narrowly centered on armaments, or the so-called Euro-group within NATO that excludes France.

During the Gulf War, Europe's record was admittedly far from substantial. (The only major contribution came from Britain, which sent 45,000 men—but even this sizable body constituted no more than 8 per cent of the total allied forces involved.) Nevertheless, WEU did some useful work in the Gulf, a region outside the direct defense area of Europe or NATO. WEU coordinated British, French, Dutch, and Italian naval forces in the Gulf. A precedent was thus set for joint European action in "out-of-area" conflicts.

The WEU's future role is as yet far from clear. France favored an independent European force to support an independent EU foreign policy. Germany wanted the best of both worlds. WEU would form the future defense arm of EU, but work in association with NATO. To Germany, this would be a way of drawing France (militarily a full member of WEU) closer to NATO, while preserving close links to the United States. Britain, Italy, the Netherlands, Portugal, and Denmark put more emphasis on NATO; they want WEU to remain subordinate to NATO rather than to constitute the core of EU's defense. From the U.S. standpoint, the British view is preferable, since the NATO alliance maximizes U.S. influence in Europe. It is also in the U.S. interest that WEU should become capable, in future, of operations outside NATO's designated areas in Europe. But whatever happens, WEU will become a major force in its own right. "It is now inconceivable to consider the defense of Europe outside the essential Alliance [WEU]."[20]

At present, WEU is in no position to replace NATO. Only NATO has the military muscle and the organizational resources to defend its members. In future, however, WEU could play a much more important part. It would be well advised to move its headquarters from Paris to Brussels, to facilitate cooperation with NATO during a ten-year transitional period. WEU might then be linked to wider regional security unions, set up within the former Warsaw Pact states and the former Soviet Union. Between them these would form a European Security Union. WEU might then take over from NATO some time in the twenty-first century. The United States should, however, continue to have a force of 100,000 or so in NATO and to preposition matériel in Europe and maintain its airlift capacity while cooperating with WEU and OSCE.

The reorganization of NATO involved wider issues of policy and command. By the mid-1990s there was almost universal agreement in Europe that the United States should remain involved there. In the United States, the principal politicians of both main parties likewise remained committed to NATO. But President Clinton, implementing plans begun under the Bush administration, reduced the U.S. presence in Europe to little over 100,000 men, thereby encouraging Europeans to take a greater part in NATO leadership.

In giving WEU a renewed role, the signatories of the Maastricht Treaty (1991) discarded two alternative options: the immediate extension of EU's competence to include defense, and that of simply "Europeanizing" NATO. In January 1993, WEU transferred its office to Brussels. At the time of writing, WEU's role was, however, not yet clear.

NATO and the New Order in East-Central Europe

The collapse of the Soviet empire revolutionized European politics. NATO also faced a host of new decisions. Should NATO simply stand fast, or should the alliance extend eastward? "Expansionists" were most prominent in the United States (which possessed a large "ethnic" lobby made up of immigrants from east-central Europe, Poles, Czechs, Croats, and others), and in Germany (linked to its eastern neighbors by historic ties of long standing). The primary candidates for admission to NATO were Poland, the Czech Republic, Slovakia, and Hungary, the "northern tier" of the east-central European states. These states were largely homogeneous in an ethnic sense (partly as a result of "ethnic cleansing" carried out during and after World War II, first by the Nazis and later by the postwar governments). Privatization had made considerable advance. (By 1994 the private sector accounted for 65 per cent of the gross domestic product in the Czech Republic, 55 per cent in Hungary, Slovakia, and Poland, as against 50 per cent in Russia and 30 per cent in Ukraine).[21] The former four countries all looked for Western support against a future resurgence of Russian imperialism. They also welcomed NATO membership as a means of maintaining internal stability. It was in the Western interest to strengthen democracy in the great border region that separated NATO's existing members from Russia. And what better time was there to extend the alliance than when Russia was weak, the Russian armed forces partly disorganized, and engaged, moreover, in putting down internal uprisings (as in Chechnya)? Russians might rail against NATO's eastward extension, but the Western powers could not afford to conduct their foreign policy subject to Moscow's veto. Thus argued hawks such as Volker Rühe, Kohl's able minister of defense, as did rea'ists within the Clinton administration, such as assistant secretary of state Richard C. Holbrooke.

The advocates of caution took a different line. They had much support within the U.S. military, and also included retired soldiers such as James M. Gavin, formerly supreme allied commander in Europe. Foreign policy experts such as Paul Nitze and George Kennan, and politicians both Republican (Pat Buchanan, a right-winger) and Democrat (Sam Nunn, a moderate) also opposed enlargement. In their view, NATO could not afford to make even more complex its already overly complex organization. To include Poles, Czechs, Slovaks, and Hungarians in the decision-making process would make NATO unmanageable. NATO could not afford to inherit new quarrels. (What would happen if, say, Hungary and Romania were to clash over Hungarian minority rights in Transylvania?) What of NATO's moral cohesion? Would Portugal wish to fight for Poland, Spain for Slovakia? To extend NATO eastward would, moreover, offend Russia. Even well-meaning Russians would regard the eastward extension as a threat at a time when the balance of even conventional forces had decisively swung in the Westerners' favor. NATO's proposed eastward extension would alienate even Russian democrats—not to speak of Russian reactionaries.[22]

Eastward extension of NATO might encourage Russia to reassert control over Belarus, Ukraine, and the Baltic states. Hence, Europe would in future be divided by a new boundary; it was folly to carry out a purely anti-Russian policy. On the contrary, Russia was needed as a great power by the West as a future counterweight against the People's Republic of China, and against militant Islam along Russia's southern marches. As Benjamin S. Lambeth, a RAND defense expert, put it, "Russia has a long-term military and strategic potential that no other country in the world besides the United States comes close to matching. America's relationship with Russia is pivotal for future international security. Our relations with other remnants of the former Soviet empire . . . will never be pivotal. . . . "[23]

At the NATO Summit in January 1994, President Clinton, to mollify Russia, proposed the Partnership for Peace (PfP), as a substitute organization linked to NATO. Twenty-six states have joined Partnership for Peace and sixteen members have military representatives in the Partnership Coordination Cell (PCC) at Mons, Belgium. Partnership for Peace activities are numerous, including military exercises, training programs, conferences/workshops, visits and other opportunities for dialogue.

The Partnership for Peace was not just a halfway house for Eastern European states such as Poland, the Czech Republic, Slovakia, and Hungary until they could qualify for full NATO membership. In fact, PfP has brought together many other countries that do not want or expect to join NATO, but whose security has improved already thanks to Partnership for Peace, even without NATO's security guarantee.[24] (By 2000 there were numerous NATO-Partnership for Peace military exercises.)

Partnership for Peace serves four purposes. It creates a dialogue between leaders of partner countries and NATO, and offers opportunities for continuous military discussions and openness to one another's defense establishments and planning process; members can have joint military operations with NATO troops and this makes NATO enlargement easier. According to U.S. Rep. Hamilton, the partnership offers countries such as Poland, the Czech Republic, and Hungary the opportunity to gain experience in cooperation with NATO, and neutral countries a chance at military cooperation without giving up their neutralism. Partnership for Peace does not draw lines to create hostile camps in Europe as during the Cold War. Political-military links have already brought better security to all partners and have helped create a new security order in Europe. NATO enlargement came in 1999; meanwhile Partnership for Peace is doing a good job in reshaping European security today. But the allies agreed that a close NATO-Russia relationship could not be subject to a Russian veto.

Reorganization of NATO

Since the end of the Cold War, NATO has been working for greater cooperation and interoperability among its members, especially with the Partnership for Peace since 1994. Interoperability in NATO is defined as the ability of systems, units, and forces to provide services and to accept services from other systems, units, and forces, and to use these services in order to operate effectively together. Even with the new Europe of PfP, however, more had to be done: training of personnel and units in NATO doctrines and practices so as to be able to work with NATO; adopting or procuring equipment that interfaces with NATO's; selecting and training of staff officers in NATO doctrines and procedures so as to be able to appoint them to staff positions in NATO or to national posts.

After the Cold War ended, NATO in 1990 issued a Declaration on Peace and Cooperation to open up cooperation with the Soviet Union and former Warsaw Pact members through the North Atlantic Cooperation Council (NACC), formed in 1991. A "Work Plan" is issued every two years covering peacekeeping, defense planning, and military matters. The NACC worked well but it was believed more was needed than dialogue and cooperation so Partnership for Peace within the NACC was set up in January 1994, at the Brussels summit.

PfP then took part in the NATO-led Implementation Force (IFOR) in Bosnia-Herzegovina. Twelve PfP nations are serving with NATO troops in IFOR. Cooperative activities in PfP now number over 700, and 20 Partnership Programs are in place with PfP members. A PfP Planning and Review Process (PARP) is being extended to advance interoperability and transparency. Fifteen nations are now working with NATO to learn about doctrines, equipment, and operations. PfP and PARP will make it easier in the future to bring new members into NATO, and for PfP members to better cooperate and operate with an enlarged NATO.

The new Europe is forcing changes not only in PfP but in NATO as well. Forces have been reduced, by 25 per cent in 1998, as have headquarters within the military structure, and a new concept was announced in 1994—the Combined Joint Task Force for collective defense in Europe as well as for new missions in out-of-area peace support operations. Russia is no longer a superpower but many risks remain. There is instability in the Balkans, in Central Asia; there is an arc of instability from Morocco to the Indian Ocean. The new structure of NATO will have to meet the future needs of an enlarged NATO and of partner nations.

A new Military Command Structure[25] has been set up to meet the new situations. The new command structure of NATO reduced the number of headquarters from 65 to 20. There will be two over-arching strategic commands (SC), one for the Atlantic, and one for Europe, with three regional commands under SC Atlantic and two under SC Europe. Component commands and Joint Sub-Regional Commands will report to Regional Commands. The aim of the new structure will be more effective performance and flexibility for all members of NATO, partner countries, and future members. The new command structures, along with implementing the Combined Joint Task Force (CJTF) concept and the development of the European Security and Defense Identity (ESDI), represents internal adaptation to allow NATO to face the challenges of the twenty-first century. The troubles arising from NATO's air war in Serbia and the occupation of Kosovo in 1999 will speed up changes in the ESDI and may well create a European security system independent of NATO.

The reshaping grew out of the London Declaration of July 1990, when NATO nations decided to meet the challenge of a new Europe. Then in 1994 a NATO Long Term Study put forward a new command structure organization, and in Berlin in 1996 it was decided to build a European Security and Defense Identity (ESDI) but also to reinforce the transatlantic partnership. While Spain joined the new military structure in 1997, France deferred—although supporting the changes and their objectives. ESDI was set up to ensure military effectiveness, preserve the transatlantic link, and develop ESDI further. All these missions were to be conducted from a single platform, NATO, capable of performing many functions. WEU is scheduled to play various roles within ESDI and even to lead some operations. The new command structure will facilitate the integration of new members and will also accommodate the expanded roles of Partnership for Peace. An Implementation Plan was aimed to activate all headquarters in the new command structure by the time of NATO's fiftieth anniversary in April, 1999.

NATO Enlargement

The NATO powers agreed on enlargement in 1998. Such a resolution was all the harder to reach because joining NATO would require larger military expenditure on the part of NATO's prospective partners; all of them would have to update their military equipment, organization, and training at a time when they all faced great budget constraints. (The Czech Republic had gone furthest in military modernization.) In any case, Western military influence had advanced eastward in an informal manner through Partnership for Peace. Poland, for example, conducted joint military maneuvers with the German *Bundeswehr*. In 1995, additional joint exercises took place in Bulgaria, Romania, Hungary, and the Czech Republic. More surprisingly still, in 1995 the United States for the first time carried out joint exercises with former reputed enemies and now members of Partnership for Peace, including Albania, Bulgaria, the Czech Republic, Croatia, Estonia, Hungary, Kyrgyzstan, Latvia, Poland, Romania, Slovenia, Ukraine, and Uzbekistan. Since 1992 the United States has also led in CJTFs operating in Eastern Europe.

In the civilian sphere, NATO in 1991 created, in Brussels, a new institution called the North Atlantic Cooperation Council (NACC). Henceforth, NATO officials would consult with various countries on a great variety of issues. (NACC met for the first time on December 20, 1991.) Prime Minister John Major tactfully described such designs as "unsettling." To push NATO to the borders of the Ukraine and Belarus might indeed be "unsettling" but necessary, if Russia falls under xenophobic nationalists and the military. NACC comprised the NATO countries and the members of the CIS, the Baltic states, the Czech Republic, Sweden, Poland, Hungary, Finland, Slovakia, Bulgaria, and Romania, providing them with new machinery for consultation.

According to former German foreign minister Hans-Dietrich Genscher, the NACC had four primary tasks: to put into effect the Treaty on Conventional Armed Forces in Europe; to ensure the security and speedy destruction of tactical nuclear weapons on CIS territory; to secure agreement for the Treaty on Non-Proliferation of Nuclear Arms from those countries that had not as yet signed; and to furnish civilian opportunities for scientists formerly engaged in research on weapons of mass destruction. The NACC discussed the Nagorno-Karabakh dispute in Azerbaijan to try to get a peace accord. Violence has continued, however, between Armenians and Azeris, and the Russians are arming the Armenians with advanced weaponry.

Three additional organizations deserve to be mentioned in discussions concerning NATO's activities. They include the CCMS (Committee on the Challenges of Modern Society, formed in 1969), a body as yet little known to the public. NATO—like the Warsaw Pact—was founded by men to whom a clear, smokeless sky over a factory town signified misery and unemployment, whereas black clouds pouring from factory chimneys meant work was once more returning to a city stricken by either an air raid or a disastrous slump. The growing ecological concerns of the 1960s had affected NATO. As early as 1969, the North Atlantic Council, then meeting in Washington, decided to give a new "social and environmental dimension" to NATO and set up the CCMS for that purpose. In 1990 the NATO summit in Brussels agreed to expand the CCMS's scope, and to invite experts from central and eastern Europe as well as from the former Soviet Union to participate in the CCMS's work. The CCMS carries out studies on environmental problems, particularly on the ecological effects of military activities. In addition, the CCMS has concerned itself with major questions such as protection against marine biological pollution, the reduction of air pollution from marine engines, pollution-prevention strategies for sustainable development, and remedial action for contaminated land and groundwater.

More ambitious still in scope was the Conference on Security and Cooperation in Europe (CSCE). The CSCE had its origins on August 1, 1975, when the Helsinki Final Act endorsed fundamental principles concerning peaceful coexistence, human rights, and constitutional government. The CSCE became the OSCE, and has held periodic meetings to consider progress regarding particular aspects of the agenda ("baskets") as defined in the Helsinki Final Act. Between major review meetings, there were formal discussions on matters such as economic cooperation, human rights, cultural cooperation, the reduction of conventional weapons, and conflict. The OSCE's organization was at first loose and informal. Yet the OSCE exerted considerable indirect influence as Soviet and other Eastern European dissidents began to appeal to the principles laid down in Helsinki—much to the Soviet authorities' annoyance.

In November 1990 the OSCE summit, held at Paris for the first time, adopted a Charter for a United Europe providing for permanent OSCE institutions. In June 1991 the Council of Foreign Ministers met at Berlin and formed the central forum for political consultation within the OSCE. Ten states within the former Soviet Union joined the OSCE. For the time being, the Council's powers did not amount to much. It could pass resolutions, and prepare for summit follow-up conferences that are held every other year. But a Committee of Senior Officials would implement resolutions, while a permanent secretariat would be responsible for administrative and public relations work. A Conflict Prevention Center in Vienna was designed to help the Council of Foreign Ministers in reducing risks of conflict. Military information would be exchanged through a specially installed communications network. A hot line would link all OSCE capitals to handle emergencies. The OSCE spanned the United States, Canada, the E.C., Yugoslavia, the former Warsaw Pact countries, and the successor states of the Soviet Union— potentially a powerful association. The OSCE provided not merely an international forum, but also a possible instrument for influencing public opinion. (For instance, in 1990, the OSCE, at a meeting in Bonn, recognized the link between a pluralistic democracy and a market economy.)

From the U.S. standpoint, the OSCE was worth backing. No matter what might be the preferences of spokesmen for a U.S. *Realpolitik*, U.S. foreign policy could not work effectively without strong support from public opinion. The OSCE did not have the UN's large bureaucracy (with its 23,000 full-time employees scattered over the globe); the OSCE did not run up the UN's big peacekeeping budget ($5.3 billion in 1993). The United States did not have any direct quarrel with any of the OSCE's members either in Western, Central, Eastern Europe, or the CIS states. The OSCE members did not promote terrorism abroad, as did UN members in good standing such as Iran and Syria. The OSCE lacked those disruptive Third World lobbies that had traditionally looked askance at the United States on the grounds that it was selfish, rich, "white," insensitive—and generally failed to provide enough aid. Neither did the OSCE suffer from that double standard of morality that for so long had beset the UN's General Assembly in dealing with the United States and its NATO allies on the one hand and the Third World on the other.

The OSCE was, however, a Cold War product. Once that war ended, the OSCE sought a wider purpose. During 1991, the OSCE could not get Yugoslavia to move to peaceful negotiations in Bosnia-Herzegovina. The group of fifty-one states had become, in President Havel's words, "a mere debating club." Havel wanted OSCE decisions to be put in treaty form and sanctions taken against those who broke the treaties. He also desired the group to have a UN-like security council and to put together peacekeeping forces. The United States and Britain opposed Havel's reforms, fearing the OSCE's trying to do things other European institutions already did. The British felt the OSCE should remain basically a political institution concerned with rule of law, human rights, and peace and should work by morally pressuring member governments. For that reason, the OSCE decided to accept the central Asian states of the CIS into membership in order to embed them in European democracy. Russia, for its part, attempted to use the OSCE as an instrument to downgrade NATO. (In 1994 Russian Defense Minister Pavel S. Grachev visited Brussels with a proposal to create a Eurasian security system headed by OSCE, not NATO. NACC would become the military arm of the new system.[26])

Once the Cold War had ended, President Bush called for a "new world order" in which the United States would play a predominant part. The American public, however, decisively rejected such an activist role; the 1992 presidential election was largely fought on domestic issues. The public seemed not to want to pay for a "new world order" at a time when the United States had so many unsolved problems at home. Isolationism had become respectable, even with impeccable Establishment members such as Richard Hyland, editor of

Foreign Affairs. Scholars such as political scientist Alexander George offered more prudent advice. The United States needs, George said, to limit its concerns and encourage free markets and trade, foster human rights, peacefully settle disputes, embargo the spread of nuclear weapons, restrict terrorists, promote democracy, strengthen mediation and peacekeeping in regional and world organizations—not withdraw from the world arena. This is a full enough agenda for the nation. Let the United States share responsibility with other regional powers and organizations—but not try to act as democracy's policeman throughout the world.

Post–Cold War Euro-American Relations

The ending of the Cold War and the loss of the "barbarians," that is, the end of the Soviet threat, has engendered unexpected challenges to the U.S.-European alliance. NATO has not been terminated; indeed it was enlarged in 1998, and U.S.-European efforts have been made in the Balkans, an out-of-area region for the old NATO. But differences have sprouted and political and economic competition has strained the Atlantic Alliance. The disputes are many: The Helms-Burton Act and the U.S.-Cuban embargo that the United States defends on the grounds of protecting human rights. The Boeing/McDonnell-Douglas merger was opposed by the Europeans and embarrassed the United States. The French softened their position against human rights abuses in China, undermining the U.S. position. There are also many disputes in the Middle East—sanctions against Iraq, Iran, the use of force against Iraq; the Americans and the Europeans disagree over forming a permanent international criminal court; finally, there continue to be disputes over Bosnia, and now Kosovo.

There have been many disputes among NATO members in the past fifty years, but some observers see the present quarrels as signaling a growing rift in transatlantic relations, not always addressed by the Alliance leaders. The rifts are not caused by the Americans' or the Europeans' loss of Alliance solidarity dating from the Cold War; rather, the shift is political and grows out of the end of the Cold War and the collapse of the Soviet Union.

During the Cold War, the Americans and the Europeans were roughly equal partners in deterring the Soviets from intimidation and attack. The United States was the superpower and provided more military hardware to NATO than did the Europeans, but the two groups benefited about equally from the relationship. "There were shared threats, shared interests and shared values in accomplishing the common goal of securing democracy and deterring aggression in Europe."[27]

With the end of the Cold War, some goals have changed. Peace-keeping, conflict resolution, and crisis management have come to the fore, overshadowing deterrence and containment. The benefits of and contributions to the Alliance are no longer equal. Bosnia is one example—the United States made the operation possible, and the United States still bears a large burden for Europe's security even though it has no national interests in Bosnia or Kosovo.

While Iraq, Iran, and North Korea affect the vital interests of the United States, Bosnia does not. The Europeans should be bearing more of the responsibilities in Kosovo and Bosnia. Americans rightly resent the Europeans' hesitancy in the Balkans, and their opposition to U.S. policies in the Middle East. Nevertheless, the Europeans protest that the United States is arrogant and acts too often without consulting them. The EU, the euro, and efforts to create a defense and foreign policy pillar are seen by some as efforts to make the Europeans independent of U.S. foreign policy. Yet Europe remains as dependent as before on the U.S. partnership, especially inside Europe.

The EU has as yet no common foreign or security policy; it does have WEU and an economic and monetary union (the euro).

Although the Europeans want to be more independent in foreign affairs, they are slashing defense budgets and reducing their conventional forces and weapons even faster than the United States. The United States is today the only Alliance member that could launch a major expeditionary force. The new NATO thus faces a contradiction: While EU is striving for unification and independence, it is also slashing defense budgets and becoming more dependent on the United States for its security. Given that the United States for six years has been cutting its budget, it is unlikely that it can sustain its global military commitments. The new strategic relationship, therefore, is unstable. Americans feel the Europeans are free riders and weaken U.S. security at times. The Europeans resent U.S. hegemony and some of its policies around the world; EU, thus, may increasingly challenge U.S. policies worldwide.

Currently, there are at least six challenges to the Atlantic Alliance:

1. The weakening credibility of President Clinton.
2. Major problems in Russia, Serbia and Kosovo, Iraq, and North Korea that have weakened the leadership position of the United States.
3. An economic crisis in the Balkans.
4. The crisis in Russia has been not just economic but political as well. Anti-American Prime Minister Putin's aggressive opposition to U.S. policies in Kosovo, the Middle East, and Europe.
5. The Iraq quagmire.
6. Peacekeeping in Kosovo.

These are some of the problems facing the United States but they are not overwhelming ones. We still have much in common with the Europeans and a fifty-year record of successful cooperation in NATO. We merely have to adjust to the post–Cold War world and to find a balance between burdens and interests, learn to cooperate and consult more openly and in a spirit of equality, not of hegemony. We are the only superpower and the great defender of freedom, democracy, security, and stability, but we need allies around the world to help us. We must lead globally in championing free trade and economic ties; we must push for a transatlantic free trade area to join the transatlantic military alliance. This military alliance must have responsibilities outside of Europe and share with the United States in globally controlling terrorism and biological and nuclear weapons.

The Continuing Debate over Enlarging NATO

The United States faced one of its major strategic challenges in this century over the issue of enlarging NATO.[28] Lessons we learned after WWI, when we withdrew precipitously from Europe, should make us realize we must stay in Europe and expand NATO's membership to former Warsaw Pact countries so as to continue to help control Germany and Russia and to keep the United States involved in Europe's affairs. This was the raison d'être for the formation of the Marshall Plan in 1947, and of NATO in 1949.

The Germans and French supported enlargement in 1998 because they wanted not only to bind Germany more closely to an integrated Europe but also to extend the NATO collective security system in the East—the area that spawned WWI, WWII, and the Cold War. Although the Germans recognized that the European Union was a long-term solution to the "German problem," they also recognized that EU, as yet, lacks a common foreign and defense policy or an armed force to deploy. The Western European Union (WEU) is still only a paper force and proved incapable of responding effectively to the 1990s crisis in Yugoslavia caused by the breakup of that state. To keep the peace in central Europe, to provide a defensive and collective security system against Russia and Yugoslavia, therefore, the enlargement of NATO was essential.

The EU, as a political and economic union, cannot guarantee the peace and security of Central and Eastern Europe and EU is no substitute for NATO enlargement as Henry Rowen and Melvyn Krauss claim. When EU is enlarged in a few years, its members, including the new ones, will be unlikely to attack each other — democratic nations that trade with one another seldom go to war with one another. But the enlargement of EU is years off; first the monetary union (EMU) has to be carried out, then Poland, Hungary, and the Czech Republic will have to conform to hundreds of laws and practices imposed on EU members. While that process goes on, NATO will be the shield against Russia and others. NATO membership by Central European nations, therefore, will help keep the peace and reduce political and diplomatic competition in the region.

An enlarged NATO will further reassure Britain and France and help contain Germany much as the original NATO did in Western Europe in 1949. Instead of worrying too much about Russia's reaction to NATO enlargement, we should remind ourselves that European politicians warn against giving Germany a free hand in the East.

NATO enlargement certainly poses problems (costs and Russia's reaction), but these are manageable. Russia's democracy will not be destroyed; Russian nationalism and xenophobia will not necessarily be ignited. Polls show Russians are mostly concerned about domestic problems, not about NATO's expansion. A bigger headache is the reaction of those states not let into NATO in this round. They must be reassured and NATO's promise of further expansion made credible. Partnership for Peace is one of the forums to use, as well as economic links with EU that will smooth the future enlargement process.

The U.S. Senate's ratification of the NATO expansion treaty in 1998 was essential to reassure the states of the former Warsaw Pact and to keep credible U.S. foreign policy in Europe. President Clinton was wrong when he talked about reducing NATO's military presence; a strong military presence will be required for some time as problems continue in the Baltics, Bosnia, and Serbia. As noted earlier, after World War II the United States formed NATO, and rearmed Germany in 1954. And after the fall of the Berlin Wall in 1989 the United States supported the quick reunification of Germany—a great strategic realignment, peacefully accomplished. But an even more difficult task remains—that is, pushing NATO's and EU's liberal democracy and mixed economy into Central Europe and beyond. This *"drang nach Osten"* of NATO can bring not only peace, but also democracy and economic development to an area that sparked two world wars in the twentieth century.

A major but seldom cited reason for supporting NATO enlargement is to make up for the Yalta sellout of 1946, which said the Soviets would occupy Central and Eastern European countries but would allow free elections. The elections were not held and all democratic institutions were suppressed. For fifty years the United States and its allies invested a great deal of manpower and money to guarantee Western European peace and security, but Warsaw Pact countries were left out. NATO enlargement will do a lot to make up for this tragedy.

The 1998 debate in the U.S. Congress was not intense—the treaty to enlarge NATO passed easily (80–19). Efforts to slow down ratification thus failed, as did efforts to limit further enlargement for three years after Poland, the Czech Republic, and Hungary were included. Other states are anxiously waiting to be asked in. Romania, Slovenia, and Bulgaria will be deeply offended and frightened if they are not included in the next round. The small Baltic states on Russia's border are even more anxious to join NATO and should be accommodated in spite of Russia's opposition to their joining. Leaving the other states out would weaken Europe's security and could threaten these nations with Russian imperialism. NATO's charter (article 10) states that NATO is open to any European state willing to adopt the principles of the treaty and to contribute to the collective security of the region. A freeze on new members now would thus hurt NATO's "flexibility and leverage." The United States "owes" the nations of Central and Eastern Europe for abandoning them at Yalta. At this time, we have to keep a positive attitude toward the future of Europe and plan to let in new members, no matter what Russia says. There are numerous organizations for Russia to express its opposition and to cooperate with: the NATO-Russian Forum, the OSCE, the Council of Europe, Partnership for Peace.

The costs of enlargement need not be a major factor. The three new states have larger military forces than Britain, Belgium, and Holland; they have old but good tanks, artillery, and planes; their military infrastructure is more than adequate—the Russians left lots of airfields, roads, army camps, and the like. The largest expense will come in modernization of forces, command and control equipment, and standardization of weapons. NATO has kept the peace in Western Europe for fifty years—it deterred the most massively armed nation in Europe, the USSR. A firm commitment by NATO, now, to defend its old as well as its new members will make up for the Yalta betrayal and ensure peace and security in Europe for the foreseeable future.[29]

The argument that NATO enlargement would anger Russia is unconvincing. Russia has no moral or political rights in the region she oppressed after World War II. Russia protested but accepted Partnership for Peace in 1994; in 1998 Russia accepted NATO enlargement and joined a NATO consultation council on military matters. The Russian people do not seem interested or worried about enlargement; only a small, xenophobic group raises its voice—for example, Vladimir Zhirinovsky and Anatoly Chubas oppose NATO enlargement, but as yet the issue has played little or no role in Russia's domestic politics. Troubles over Kosovo flared up in 1999 and NATO's enlargement to the east was forgotten.

In any case, the Russian state is ill-prepared to launch adventurous forays to its west; however, the states on Russia's border that suffered under Russian rule see a well-armed Russian military; they therefore have a legitimate concern about the future. NATO membership can assuage their fears, check Russian ambitions, and bring collective security to a region torn by bloody turmoil twice in the twentieth century. Remember, NATO kept the Russians out of Western Europe after World War II when the USSR was the most militarized society in the world. An enlarged NATO, including states once ravaged and dominated by communism, committed to a defensive posture and to peacekeeping, not warmaking, can do it again.

Senator Sam Nunn, on the floor of the U.S. Senate, October 10, 1995, argued forcefully that NATO enlargement would anger Russian nationalists and isolate Russian democrats and reformers. Although Russia lacks the resources to respond to NATO enlargement with a conventional military buildup at the present time, Nunn fears that if nationalists come to power they might further build up and deploy tactical nuclear forces. Security in Eastern Europe is not enhanced by NATO enlargement, the Senator claims, especially "if the Russian military finger moves closer to the nuclear trigger."

A hawk during the Cold War, Nunn now fears alienating Russia and encouraging not democrats but nationalists and former Communist imperialists. He does not believe we can convince the East Europeans that we are protecting them from Russia, their historical enemy, while convincing the Russians that NATO enlargement is not aimed at Russia. And how can we expect Russia to let the Baltic countries on its borders join NATO? Nunn asks, "How about the Ukraine and Belarus, anxious to rejoin Russia? Are we deluding others, or are we deluding ourselves?"

Although Senator Nunn fears isolating Russia and provoking some kind of nuclear buildup to meet the conventional challenge posed by NATO, he does not argue that Russia is justified in opposing NATO expansion. Susan Eisenhower, president of the Center for Political and Strategic Studies, did, in her arguments before the Senate Budget Committee, on Oct. 29, 1997. From the Russian standpoint, she argues, "there are grievances." Russians feel they did the most and suffered the most in World War II, and are justified in fearing invasion from the West, and now they face a former enemy, Germany, in a NATO expanding to the east and incorporating Russia's former Warsaw Pact allies.

Furthermore, Eisenhower asserts, Russia feels it "ended" communism, lost its superpower status, and terminated the Cold War on terms now being disregarded: that NATO would not expand eastward, that Warsaw Pact states would not join NATO, and that the Baltic states were to be given independence only after they promised to remain neutral. Eisenhower claims that the Russians would never have agreed to German reunification if they had thought it would lead to NATO's expansion. On this point, as on many others, Eisenhower is wrong. The Soviet Union refused to come to East Germany's defense when crowds assembled in 1989 to protest against the East German Communist regime. The Communist government fell, the wall came down, and the Warsaw Pact disintegrated. Premier Gorbachev had no control over events after he refused to back the leader of East Germany, Honecker, in putting down the popular uprisings—Soviet troops stayed in their barracks. German reunification was up to the West, not the East, but was agreed to by the Russians. President George Bush quickly settled the matter by supporting Chancellor Kohl's efforts to reunite Germany. A reunited Germany was accepted in NATO, but NATO's expansion to East Germany was not part of any debate between the old Cold War antagonists. Nor did Russia have any right to tell sovereign nations not to join NATO. These former victims of Communist oppression have now asked to join the alliance. How can they be denied?

In the United States, a left-right coalition, the Coalition Against NATO Expansionism (CANE), failed to stop Poland, Hungary, and the Czech Republic from joining NATO, but it may well remain a major force opposing further enlargement and U.S. internationalism. CANE brought together two groups—left-wing universalists and right-wing isolationists. The CANE founders were John Isaacs and William Lind, friends at Dartmouth College in the 60s. Lind joined the hard-right Free Congress Foundation and Isaacs ran the Council for a Liveable World Education Fund, a peace group. They both opposed NATO and NATO expansion and put together a group of strange bedfellows: the Eagle Forum, the conservative American Defense Institute (hawks), Melvyn Krauss of the Hoover Institution, and the Cato Institute (libertarian), from the right. From the left came Peace Action, the Union of Concerned Scientists, and the Center for Defense Information—all opposing U.S. military spending and foreign entanglements. The left was at least consistent with its earlier Cold War views, that is, with its opposition to U.S. military action overseas, but now it preaches a universalism for exporting democracy and peacekeeping. It opposes the expansion of NATO because Russia is not included! But the right opposes NATO enlargement on the grounds that the United States cannot export democracy, and Eastern Europe will involve the United States in the chronic feuds of the region. Cato and Krauss say enlargement will cost too much and allow the Europeans to spend more on welfare and less on security. The Cato Institute (and Krauss, too) want the United States to retreat into isolationism. (Krauss calls it unilateral globalism. He wants the United States to end all "entangling alliances" and to pull out of Europe, Korea, and Japan.) The best solution, according to CANE, is to divide the continent along regional lines (as in the Cold War). Recognize a Russian sphere of influence and let Germany dominate in Central Europe. Sound familiar? The right has again become isolationist—if the United

States is not directly threatened, stay out of Europe's quarrels and do not pay for Europe's welfare system by letting it off the hook for spending on defense. And the left retains its anti-internationalism and anti-capitalism.

CANE's and Cato's arguments did not win in the Senate, but their quirky ideas may well surface again. CANE and Cato will continue to oppose NATO enlargements, the Asia bailout, and as the left and right did in the Cold War, they will wreck U.S. internationalism—the left because it does not go far enough, and the right because it does not want the United States to be the policeman of the world, or to support and enter regional alliances such as NATO or the United States–Japan security treaty. Coalitions such as CANE do not offer viable or coherent alternatives; they merely expose an incoherent populist rage and isolationist tendencies.[30]

NATO's New Members

NATO enlargement is important to Poland, Hungary, and the Czech Republic—formerly in the Warsaw Pact. They see it as protection from Russia and as a return to a traditional European alliance. Being in NATO will not only help them promote stability and prosperity in Europe, but will also encourage peace, democracy, and economic development in their own countries. (They also have applied to join EU.) An enlarged NATO adds military resources to the alliance, and protects Western interests and those of the states of Central Europe against future threats. A deeper purpose of enlargement is to safeguard Western interests and cultures connected by a common history and Euro-American civilization. Nevertheless, some critics of expansion question whether NATO is still important for U.S. security.

For this writer, NATO expansion was necessary to consolidate the zone of peace and democracy in Europe. It removed a security vacuum in Central Europe, in an area where conflict led to World Wars I and II. It will provide new members and the alliance with insurance against a revived, xenophobic Russia. It will enhance NATO's military capabilities at a reasonable cost. Since the end of the Warsaw Pact, the region has been unstable and needs NATO membership to reassure its members that the United States will remain in Europe and help to keep Germany as well as Russia under control. The United States, for its national interests, should stay involved in Europe to ensure a balance of power there, but should make the Europeans pay a larger share of the costs of defense and enlargement.

If NATO doesn't expand, some experts argue, it could well dissolve. The United States would then pull back to isolationism and cut its ties with Europe. To avoid such a withdrawal, collective security through NATO needs to be spread to Central and Eastern Europe, but not by Germany alone. The credibility of the United States as an ally would have been undermined if new members had not been accepted.

According to the RAND Corporation, the costs of enlargement to NATO are moderate—$10 to $15 billion over ten years. (The Congressional Budget office estimates the cost at $125 billion over ten years.) The U.S. share of the costs is estimated by the RAND Corporation at $400 million a year—a small sum for ensuring peace and collective security in Europe, the source of U.S. civilization and its second largest trading partner. Furthermore, the costs of sustaining a force to prevent war would be much less than those of fighting a war. The potential expense of failing to expand eastward is, therefore, great—it would create a security vacuum in Central and Eastern Europe; it would also create dangerous geopolitical pressures vis-à-vis Germany, Central Europe, and Russia.

In any case, the real costs are to be shared equitably. The costs of improving the infrastructure are relatively small because of the presence of large numbers of former Warsaw Pact camps, supply

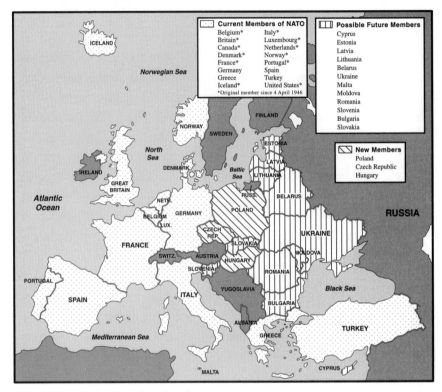

MAP 2   NATO Looks Ahead

depots, roads, airfields, and equipment. In addition, there is a large manpower pool to draw on—for example, in Poland, with over 200,000 troops. The new states are now being given older equipment by other NATO members, and U.S. army/airforce teams are training personnel throughout Central and Eastern Europe. A Polish or Czech soldier costs much less than a Western European or American soldier.

In addition to supporting NATO's recent enlargement, the United States since 1992, through NATO, has been exporting U.S. military doctrine and training to more than two dozen countries.

Countries request this training in order to be linked to the West and to be trained by the West, whether or not they get into NATO or PfP. Thirteen countries in Central and Eastern Europe are at present receiving U.S. military training through the Combined Joint Task Force (CJTF), and plans call for the extension of the program into the Caucasus and the newly independent states on the border of Russia. In Europe the aim of CJTF is to create a security zone across Eastern Europe. (But the program covers the world and touches at least 110 countries as part of a peacetime engagement, according to the Pentagon.) The CJTF program costs about $20 million a year and sends four- or five-man teams to defense ministries and to general staff offices in thirteen nations in Eastern Europe. In 1998, 1,400 U.S. military personnel went to the region to help train 100,000 troops, and 1,400 Eastern European officers came to the United States or to bases in Europe for classroom training and seminars. The joint chiefs of staff under Colin Powell started the program in 1992 after the end of the Cold War. To avoid Congressional budget fights, the DoD called the U.S. experts "exchanges" and "contact teams" rather than trainers. Most of the exchanges, therefore, are not on the Pentagon budget; they are listed as on "temporary duty." Hundreds of National Guard staffers are included in the program. In many ways the CJTF is more effective than the State Department as an on-site agent of U.S. foreign policy. The State Department is small, underfunded, and understaffed. The U.S. military has what these countries want—the infrastructure and educational programs to train people in NATO military tactics and organization.

By 1999, the CJTF had done full-scale assessments of armed forces in Lithuania, Latvia, Estonia, Bulgaria, and Romania, and designed plans to remodel the military of the Czech Republic, Poland, Hungary, Romania, and Slovenia. For five countries, the United States and NATO have installed computers for budgeting and acquisition systems; they have drafted military codes and taught tactical war-fighting doctrines. Such work is most advanced in the three countries recently admitted to NATO; however, in some former Communist countries such as Bulgaria, the CJTF has not worked well because of government suspicion and Communist tradition.

The CJTF work in Lithuania stresses small-unit tactics. The Lithuanian army has modeled itself on U.S. command and security structure, and its training and doctrine is based on U.S. Army rules. The Lithuanian government increased its military spending by 50 percent in 1993. A U.S. seven-man CJTF team has worked out of Vilnius since the Russians left in 1993. There have been numerous military exchanges; combat training and special operations units have taught the Lithuanians long-range reconnaissance and surveillance techniques.

As noted earlier, Partnership for Peace was the first medium for the United States to act in Eastern Europe before states joined NATO. The PfP also has held military exercises and sought to bring PfP member countries up to NATO standards. PfP and the CJTF are still dominated by the United States in their agenda and budgets.

Not everybody agrees with the CJTF's mandate. Some fear that Russia will react badly to the U.S. presence on its borders, or that the CJTF will allow the military to dominate the new democracies. Others resent the cost of modernizing their country's military, and fear that it will detract from developing the economies and social programs of these recently Communist states. The Czech critics fear the expense but also worry about a regional arms race. The United States in 1998 gave $120 million in military equipment to the region, and states that got little may pressure for more.

Proponents of the CJTF counter all these arguments: Russian acceptance has been won because Russia is in PfP, and is consulted and told of all military training exercises. The United States is not encouraging an arms race but is trying to discourage most countries from large defense purchases. The NATO allies are helping

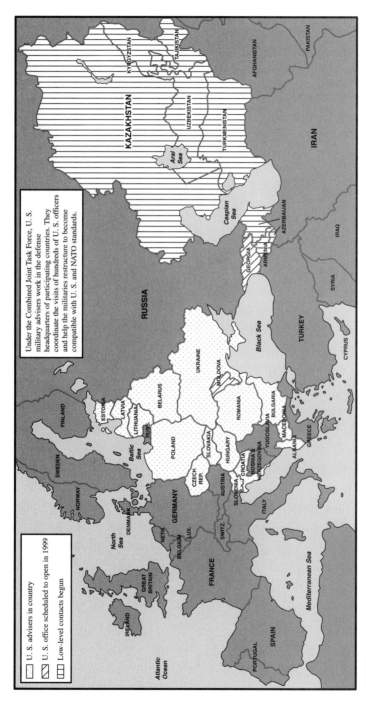

Under the Combined Joint Task Force, U. S.
military advisers work in the defense
headquarters of participating countries. They
coordinate the visits of hundreds of U. S. officers
and help the militaries restructure to become
compatible with U. S. and NATO standards.

U. S. advisers in country
U. S. office scheduled to open in 1999
Low-level contacts begun

MAP 3 Peacetime Engagement: U.S. Military on a New Frontier

"NATOize" the new democracies by giving them older equipment and by training, so costs should be kept manageable. In any case, trade and investment will follow when local military systems are beefed up and linked to NATO and PfP. Membership in EU will also bring even more trade and investment to the region.

As noted earlier, fear of Russia's opposition to NATO enlargement should not be taken lightly, but it should not deter enlargement or use of PfP or CJTF. The majority of Russians don't care about Poland, the Czech Republic, and Hungary joining NATO; they are worried about wages, jobs, and medical care at home. The Russian right forced a peace settlement in Chechnya and now have no stomach for sending their sons to fight to get the Baltic states back. Some Russian leaders do warn against NATO extending into the Baltic area, but only time will tell what, if anything, they can do about such peaceful expansion. Russian responses to the Yugoslav imbroglio were not reassuring, however.

The end of the Cold War did not mean, as some claim, that NATO had lost its reason for being. To repeat, NATO was formed to keep the Russians out, the Germans down, and the Americans involved in Europe. In spite of the demise of the Soviet Empire and the Warsaw Pact, Europe is still a dangerous place, still in need of the unique safeguard that NATO, led by the United States, can offer. Opponents of expansion forget NATO is a defensive alliance (and since the 1990s a peacekeeping, not primarily a war-fighting organization). New members do not need expensive aircraft to attack Russia's army or big tanks to lead an offensive against Russia. All the new members of NATO can supply people for the defense of their homelands and for many peacekeeping jobs in the Balkans and elsewhere. For all these tasks, the new members of NATO need command and control equipment for communication, defensive equipment such as antitank weapons and artillery. The CJTF and PfP are modernizing their forces as well as training them in NATO military and peacekeeping tactics. There are plenty of troops and bases to use for defensive purposes. NATO can use its close support aircraft to repel the Russian army, and bombers to attack the Russian army's rear if necessary. The advanced equipment is in NATO or German bases, and doesn't have to be supplied to Poland or Hungary or based there.

Until recently, Russia appeared compliant, although critical of NATO enlargement. Russia had been a member of Partnership for Peace since 1994, and signed, in 1997, the "Founding Act on Mutual Relations, Cooperation and Security between NATO and the Russian Federation." Russia had had a voice in the Council but no veto. It seemed that Russia was mollified and that an expanded NATO would be able to carry out its core missions of peacekeeping, war prevention, and conciliation. But with the air war over Serbia that began in March 1999, Russia once again took a stridently anti-NATO stance.

To conclude, the new NATO allies (Poland, the Czech Republic, and Hungary) are a boon to NATO and the United States. NATO created a bridge between Europe and the United States, and this bridge will be expanded further with the addition of the three states of Central Europe. This will then define the Atlantic Alliance and the Atlantic identity from Alaska to Turkey. When NATO began in 1949 it involved only nations in Western Europe, former allies and foes alike, who shared common interests and a common culture. NATO was the basis for a Euro-American partnership and the primary institution for collective security during the Cold War. In the post–Cold War world, with its defensive mission accomplished, NATO has now to expand security to the East, a region still potentially dangerous and unstable. The EU, WEU, and OSCE were unable to stop the war in Bosnia; only NATO created some stability in the shattered Yugoslav federation and is trying to impose peace and a sense of collective security in the Balkan region, a historic cockpit of struggle. Since the Warsaw Pact and the USSR disintegrated, NATO has been able to offer some stability to the newly freed states. All of this has served the national interests of all members of NATO.

The primary functions of NATO today and tomorrow are peace-keeping, crisis management, conflict resolution, and encouraging cooperation among the community of states that make up the European continent. The air strikes over Kosovo have raised the costs to NATO and led to war-fighting, humanitarian interventionism, and now peacekeeping in Kosovo. The risks of a break with Russia are great, even though Russia brokered the agreement with Slobodan Milosevic, president of Yugoslavia.

Finally, NATO expansion carries the Atlantic partnership to the East and belatedly fulfils our pledge made at Yalta to the states of Central and Eastern Europe, relinking them to Western civilization. It also keeps us engaged in Europe and bolsters the alliance in that historically war-torn area.[31]

Part IV

The Yugoslav Imbroglio

The NATO powers have been divided over the Yugoslav imbroglio since 1989. President Bush initially feared the multiplication of small ethnic states; he had at first no more desire to see Yugoslavia break up than to witness the dissolution of the Soviet Union. Britain, France, Spain, all had separatists at home—respectively in Scotland and Northern Ireland, the Bretagne and Corsica, Catalonia and the Basque lands. Hence they were far from enthusiastic about Yugoslavia's threatened collapse in 1991. Germany, however, had different priorities. The ruling Christian Democratic Union (more particularly the Christian Social Union, the CDU's Bavarian sister party), sympathized with fellow Catholics in Croatia. Germans of whatever religious persuasion felt that the right of self-determination, so recently claimed by Germans in the German Democratic Republic, should not be withheld from Croatians or Slovenes. More particularly, Chancellor Kohl and his former Foreign Minister Dietrich Genscher, a Liberal Democrat, wished to reassert united Germany's might in Europe. Germany thus quickly recognized Croatia's and Slovenia's independence. Thereafter Macedonia also broke away from Yugoslavia, followed at the end of 1991 by Bosnia-Herzegovina. In Macedonia, Macedonians uneasily coexisted with Albanians, Serbs, Turks, Bulgars, and Gypsies. But ethnic strife was contained, at least for the time being, and Macedonia received international recognition in spite of Greek opposition.

In 1989 President Slobodan Milosevic stripped Kosovo of its autonomy, held since 1974, and sent in troops to stop the protests of ethnic Albanians. Then in 1991 Secretary of State James Baker tried to restrain Serbia after Slovenia and Croatia declared independence. The United States warned Milosevic about any further violence against Kosovo Albanians. Brutal war and ethnic cleansing followed. In Bosnia-Herzegovina, by contrast, secession led to bitter and prolonged hostilities for three years. Had Bosnia-Herzegovina agreed to stay within the boundaries of rump Yugoslavia (now composed only of Serbia and Montenegro), war might have been avoided. But once Bosnia-Herzegovina had broken away, the Bosnian Serbs in turn sought independence from a Muslim-dominated government, and set up their own republic, supported by Serbia proper. The Bosnian Croats wavered between supporting and opposing the Bosnian government. Both Croats and Serbs engaged in "ethnic cleansing" (the Croats in Croatia and Krajina, the Serbs in Bosnia). All three combatants raised substantial forces—costly to equip, expensive to maintain, a burden for every economy. These military wings resembled one another in their composition—regulars, genuine volunteers, more or less reluctant conscripts, and a motley crew of adventurers and thugs who looted for profit and raped for fun. It was these paramilitary soldiers who committed the bulk of the numerous atrocities. But for the Serbs in particular "ethnic cleansing" proved a disastrous mistake from the viewpoint of *realpolitik* as well as of morality.

The Bosnian crisis not only exacerbated traditional ethnic hostilities, but also reopened long-standing cleavages in international affairs. Germany, as we have seen, once more supported Croatia, formerly part of the Austro-Hungarian empire. Greece and Russia backed their fellow Orthodox believers in Serbia. Greece, for a time, imposed a blockade on Macedonia, whose very name supposedly formed a threat to Greek Macedonia, and Russia supported fellow orthodox Slavs and defended Serbs against NATO and the UN. Turkey sided with its fellow Muslims in Albania and Bosnia, and so did Turkey's rival, Iran, which supplied the Bosnian Muslims with weapons.

The UN responded by sending "peacekeepers" to Bosnia as part of a so-called United Nations Protection Force (UNPROFOR), NATO supplying the military muscle. Their task was to protect minorities caught behind enemy lines, supply food to starving civilians, and protect so-called safe areas. Despite an international embargo, the entire region was awash with arms. Given the size of the contending Slav forces, UNPROFOR was too small and too heterogeneous to dominate the situation. Worse still, NATO's support was half-hearted. (The United States provided only air and naval support. The *Bundeswehr*, committed, at long last, to intervention in 1995, only furnished military aircraft, air transport, and field hospitals.)

As noted earlier, to solve the Yugoslav conundrum, President Clinton in 1995 had suggested a compromise that allotted 51 per cent of Bosnia-Herzegovina to a Croat-Muslim federation, and 49 per cent to the Bosnian Serbs within a federal state. Bosnia remained an internationally recognized state, with its borders intact. Each of the two constituent regions would enjoy self-government, with its own constitution. Each region would be allowed to form "parallel special relationships" respectively with neighboring Croatia and Serbia.

Under heavy U.S. pressure, a peace accord was signed in Dayton, Ohio, in 1995. Peace was to be assured for a time by a powerful NATO force numbering about 60,000 men, mostly American, British, and French. These forces would stay for at least a year and separate the combatants from one another. Civil administration would be left to the OSCE (Organization for Security and Cooperation in Europe). Headed by Ambassador Robert Frowick, an American, the OSCE Mission comprised an international staff of 250 persons. They would supervise elections, monitor human rights, facilitate arms control, and conduct negotiations on security-building—a Herculean task.

By that time, of course, Yugoslavia's successor states were in desperate trouble. An estimated 2,000,000 to 3,000,000 people had

MAP 4   Bosnian Settlement, 1996

been driven from their homes. Misery was rife and so was violence, both official and unofficial. Nevertheless, there were both winners and losers. The chief winner was Croatia. Supported by the United States, Croatia had built a strong army, and created a Greater Croatia. Among other territories, the Croats had reconquered the Krajina from the indigenous Serbs. (The Croats thereby set off a great exodus of refugees without, however, thereby incurring the same international stigma that beset the Serbs.) The Muslim-Croat federation, created within Bosnia at U.S. urging (in 1994), seemed a fragile entity. To all intents and purposes, its Croat component joined Croatia.

After the Bosnian peace agreement was signed in Paris on December 14, 1995, a NATO-led multinational implementation force (IFOR) was created. IFOR's primary tasks were to:

Ensure compliance with the cease-fire
Ensure troop withdrawals to the respective territories
Collect heavy weapons and demobilize forces
Control air space over Bosnia-Herzegovina

IFOR was important for the transition to peace in the first year of the Dayton peace agreement. IFOR helped the OSCE in the task of preparing for the election of September 14, 1996. IFOR also repaired roads and bridges, and restored gas, water, and electricity connections as well as telecommunication channels. Under IFOR schools and hospitals were rebuilt. Having provided a secure environment, IFOR was replaced by a stabilization force (ISOR) on December 20, 1996, to further ensure the peace process, and to help create a single, democratic and multiethnic state. An uneasy peace has prevailed in Bosnia. Many refugees were not allowed to return to their homes, but at least the killing stopped and NATO peacekeepers are likely to occupy Bosnia for some years.

Bosnia was finally divided between Croats, Serbs, and Bosnian Muslims, but one area, Brcko, was set between the Serb Republika Srpska, half in Bosnia-Herzegovina and half in Yugoslavia. In 1996 U.S. troops had been sent to Bosnia but President Clinton promised to have them out in a year. That promise was not kept because of continuing tensions and trouble there and in Kosovo. Kosovo presented a different problem. Serbia has ruled Kosovo; sovereignty was not divided as in Bosnia. Ethnic hatred is great in Kosovo, which is still part of Yugoslavia, and violence and attacks on Serbs and occupied villages by the Kosovo Liberation Army (KLA) intensified in 1998.

After much wrangling, peace talks at the end of 1998 in Rambouillet near Paris had tried to find a practical settlement between Kosovo province and Serb-ruled Yugoslavia. NATO threatened air strikes to stop Serb violence against the people of Kosovo if talks failed. The United States offered 4,000 peacekeeping troops for the area. The U.S. ambassador to Macedonia, Christopher Hill, was in charge of negotiations. The ethnic Albanians of Kosovo were badly divided; one group, the Democratic League of Kosovo led by President-elect Ibrahim Rugova, wanted autonomy within Yugoslavia, and the other, a hard-line guerilla group, the Kosovo Liberation Army (KLA), wanted independence. The Armed Forces of the Republic of Kosovo, an exiled group under Bujar Bukoshi, opposed the others.

The West kept pressure on Milosevic. The contact group for the former Yugoslavia (United States, France, Britain, Russia) aimed to force the Serbs to accept an autonomous Kosovo, as it had been ten years earlier, before Milosevic came to power. The Rambouillet Kosovo Peace Plan for the ethnic Albanians and the Yugoslav government would have granted Kosovo limited self-rule with a NATO peacekeeping force to impose the agreement. The people would have elected their own government and taken charge of police, education, trade, economic development, and the justice system, and in three years would have voted for independence or autonomy within Yugoslavia. The Yugoslav government would have kept control of defense, foreign policy, federal taxes and customs, but the Serbs rejected the agreement and NATO air strikes began on March 24, 1999.

Kosovo was thus more ambiguous than Bosnia. Both areas have seen human horror and refugee flights. The Serbs were the aggressors in both places, but the Serbs have some legitimate arguments in their claim to Kosovo. Though once autonomous, Kosovo was still part of Yugoslavia, and the Serbs resisted Kosovo's cries for independence. Riots and violence had broken out in the 1980s, until in 1989 Yugoslav authorities further lessened Kosovo's autonomy. The struggle continued, however; in 1990 the Kosovars declared independence, and in 1991 established the Republic of Kosovo. In 1992 Ibrahim Rugova was elected president; he has continuously called for a Kosovo independent of Serbia and Albania. But Albania is a major player in the region, because 90 per cent of Kosovars are ethnic Albanians. Trade between Albania and Serbia continues, even an arms trade, and most of the refugees from Kosovo fled to Albania. In the refugee camps the KLA recruited and trained young men and women for the return to Kosovo. The KLA is associated with a drive for a Greater Albania—that is, to include Albania, parts of Macedonia, and Kosovo—and this, of course, the Serbs resist. A low-level civil war was always likely in NATO-held Kosovo between the KLA, Serbs, and KFOR troops trying to impose a peace settlement.

For some Serbs, the loss of Kosovo would mean the death of their Serb civilization and the loss of the seat of Serb nationalism. For thousands of Serbs living in Kosovo it means they will become refugees, as were the ethnic Albanians. The northern part of the province is also resource-rich and provides a vital road and access to the sea through Montenegro, part of the Yugoslav Republic. All sides in the dispute have made mistakes and the people of Kosovo have paid a heavy price—thousands dead, 900,000 or so refugees, scores of villages, towns, and cities destroyed. But the Serbs, too, suffered—economic boycotts and air assaults on their cities and infrastructure, and Serbs were displaced as ethnic Albanians returned to Kosovo.

Montenegro is also at risk from Milosevic's rump Yugoslav federation. Under President Milos Djukanovic since 1997, Montenegro is a de facto independent state. It has an elected parliament and a multiethnic government. Refugees from Kosovo flooded into Montenegro as well as Macedonia and Albania. Belgrade also threatened Djukanovic with military intervention. Unrest was imminent,

as Milosevic called up conscripts for Kosovo. This could have destabilized the entire region—hurt civil society in Serbia, encouraged
Serbs in Bosnia, and put at risk NATO's mission in Kosovo. There
was, and is, a need in Montenegro, as in Kosovo, to deter Milosevic's
aggression. The United States needed to draw a red line around
Montenegro and not dilly-dally as it had done in Kosovo.

Politics in Kosovo

The air war shattered the political ranks of the Kosovars and divided the
resistance forces. Some Kosovar leaders went into hiding, others were
killed, and the KLA forces broke up and were driven to hide in the
mountains or take refuge in Albania or Macedonia. Ibrahim Rugova,
previously the most prominent advocate of Kosovar autonomy, was no
longer trusted—he was accused of selling out to Milosevic. The West
continued to court Rugova as he traveled around Europe seeking support for his Democratic League of Kosovo.

The Kosovar factions were united at Rambouillet but are now at
odds with each other again, and the time and place for talks has yet
to be set. Rugova's main rival is Hashim Thaci (Thaqi), chief of the
KLA and the appointed prime minister of Kosovo. Thaci leads the
younger, more militant Kosovar generation. These militants pose a
hard challenge for NATO: Wanting full independence soon, the
militants have opposed Kosovo's return to Serb control and have
been slow to disarm fully.

The Armed Forces of the Republic of Kosovo (AFRK) were
trained in the summer of 1998 in North Kosovo under the direction
of the exiled leader Bujar Bukoshi, who had been the de facto rep-
resentative of ethnic Albanians living in Europe. The KLA and
AFRK have been rival movements in the struggle for Kosovo independence, and this has hurt cooperation between their military
wings, but some joint activities have been reported recently.

The Kosovo Liberation Army first appeared in the Bosnian conflict in 1992; some 5,000 ethnic Albanians, allied with Croat and Bosnian Muslim forces, fought against Serbia. When the question of autonomy for Kosovo was ignored in the Dayton peace accords of 1995, the KLA began to attack Serb police forces, but not military units, in Kosovo. The KLA drew its trained cadres from the Yugoslav army and the State Security Service. The force largely consists of Kosovars, but also includes some 1,000 foreign mercenaries who arrived after the air campaign against Yugoslavia began. Some instructors were from the United Kingdom and Germany. The KLA tactics changed in 1998 from hit-and-run attacks on Serb units to large-scale action to hold villages and to disrupt communication between local Serb troops. In 1999, before the bombing campaign, Serb forces intensified their efforts against the KLA troops and largely dispersed them. The KLA then fought from the mountains and along the borders.

The military wing of the KLA pushed a corridor into Kosovo from northern Albania, but mostly its forces existed in enclaves and on the move as guerilla groups along the borders. They were outgunned, fought mostly at night, but survived—guerillas don't have to win; they only have to survive. Overall, the KLA lacked competent leadership and political unity between the various units, did not coordinate its attacks, and lacked experienced fighters. The Albanian army also helped the KLA, as did NATO airpower and the threat of invasion, but in the end diplomacy and NATO airpower forced the Serbs out of Kosovo.

The KLA is made up of peasants, Marxists, dissidents, bandits, criminal gangs, and students. Serb attacks on the people of Kosovo enabled the KLA to win over both the general population and the Kosovar elite in 1997–1999 and to establish a shadow administration to govern Kosovo. The Kosovar elite, however, feared control by the KLA. They worried that the KLA, Marxism, and criminal elements would dominate Kosovo when the Serbs left. The political elite, however, had no organization to put in place against the well-organized KLA. NATO, too, faced problems with the KLA: After cooperating with it to fight the Serbs, NATO had to disarm it. Although NATO wanted the Serbs to continue living in the new Kosovo, it feared a KLA vendetta against the Serbs. These fears were realized and thousands of Serbs have fled.

Conducting the Air War in Kosovo

Since the implosion of the Soviet Union, Russian attitudes toward the West have become increasingly hostile and resentful. In spite of vast sums in aid and loans, much advice, and consultation and cooperation in security plans for Europe, the Russian elite seems to believe the West wants to reduce Russia to a third-rate power. To Westerners, such attitudes are as baffling as their consequences are obstructionist. Russia demands to be treated as a great power, engages with anti-West nations, and refuses to cooperate with the West. But Russia did broker a deal in Yugoslavia.

The Russians were infuriated by the air war against the Serbs. They viewed it not only as an attack on a long-term ally and coreligionist but as a direct threat to their own security and an insult to their position as a world power. They first threatened the West and then intervened diplomatically to bring an end to the war. President Yeltsin, in May–June 1999, sent his former prime minister, Viktor Chernomyrdin, on a mediation tour of the West, China, and Serbia to work out a "deal" to save Serbia. The West finally accepted much of the Russian plan. The plan approved by NATO, the G-8 group, and the UN Security Council made Russia a player in Balkan politics.

Although Kosovo had seen the hottest clash between Russia and the West since Cold War days, the negotiations produced most of what NATO wanted. All Serb police and military had to leave, all refugees would return, and Kosovo province remained within the

Yugoslav republic. But NATO had clearly underestimated both Milosevic's determination to hold Kosovo and Russia's support for the Serbs. The final agreement was possible only because NATO did not insist on a vote after three years on autonomy as the Rambouillet Accord had called for.

The Balkan crisis, once again, demonstrated that Russia is difficult to integrate into the Western political and economic system. Russia is a Eurasian power and always has been. Its national interests and its points of view are not compatible with the West's. The West should accept this stark fact, but it should keep trying to cooperate with Russia, seek a partnership whenever possible, but not expect the Russians to change into a Western nation and an ally.

The air war over Kosovo and Serbia was waged essentially for political and humanitarian reasons. Public support from NATO's eighteen members was essential, which imposed severe political constraints on NATO's leadership. The ambassadors at the North Atlantic Council (NAC) in Brussels each day had to approve bombing targets and various military details, as did senior officials in some capitals. President Clinton had to approve each tactical change in the air war. The supreme allied commander in Europe, General Wesley A. Clarke, repeatedly let it be known that basic rules of warfare were being ignored to keep the political cohesion of the alliance. In future wars a different decision-making procedure will have to replace unanimous decisions.

The ethnic cleansing of Kosovo was carefully planned by the Yugoslav army and the Interior Ministry and was carried out by various Serb forces under a single command. The operation had at least two goals: defeating the KLA rebellion and changing the ethnic balance of Kosovo by driving out the Albanians. By May 1999, 90 per cent of all ethnic Albanians had been expelled from their homes in Kosovo—about 900,000 fled across Kosovo's borders and more than 500,000 were refugees inside Kosovo. It was thought about ten thousand people were killed during this time; no such figures have yet been corroborated. But claims of genocide and ethnic cleansing shocked world opinion and allowed NATO to launch the war.

The KLA had been fighting a not very intense guerilla war since 1993. The Serbs aimed to restrict its base of support by expelling the ethnic Albanians along carefully controlled corridors on the main highways. In isolating the KLA, the Serbs believed they could destroy it in the fields and mountains. The campaign was stepped up soon after NATO's first bombs fell. The overall purpose of the campaign, then, was to attack KLA strongholds and to depopulate Kosovo by expelling ethnic Albanians from Priština and other large cities so the Serbs could control the region and settle hundreds of thousands of Serbs from lost territory in Croatia and Bosnia.

President Clinton had repeatedly stated in 1999 that he did not intend to put ground troops into Kosovo and that an air war would bring the Serbs to the table. Prime Minister Tony Blair, on the other hand, from the beginning had been an outspoken advocate of an invasion. Domestic pressure had been mounting on President Clinton to launch a ground war, and he finally answered that he had not ruled out that option. Neither the joint chiefs nor Defense Secretary William Cohen favored a ground war. But the joint chiefs saw the value of such a threat to force Milosevic to surrender, and many NATO officials criticized Clinton for ruling out a general invasion when the air war started. Clinton again was forced to ask Blair to stop pushing for a ground war.

But the air war did not weaken the Serbs and created vast refugee flows. Blair in mid-April again called for a ground war to defeat Milosevic. In meetings with Clinton, Prime Minister Blair and top NATO officials in mid-April began to discuss an invasion, and General Clark, the NATO commander, was told to plan a ground invasion. Clark came up with a plan, and Clinton approved positioning forty-five thousand NATO troops in Macedonia to serve as the core of an invasion force. (In early June Blair had committed thirty thousand reservists to such an invasion.) Then on June 2, the day before President Slobodan Milosevic accepted NATO's terms to end the war, the Clinton administration held a long meeting of national security officials to discuss how NATO could win the war. The White House was looking for options that did not require an invasion by up to 175,000 troops as suggested by General Clark.

The bombing campaign had been stepped up to include bridges, roads, heating plants, and electric power stations. To everyone's surprise the strategy worked; on June 3 the Serb leader accepted NATO's terms. The bombs had had little effect in Kosovo because of camouflage and mock bridges and tanks, but the Russians and Finns had helped convince Milosevic that more extensive bombing was coming and, most important, that NATO was preparing a ground invasion. Furthermore, Milosevic had won some important concessions from NATO: The United Nations, not NATO, would control the peace accords and Kosovo; Kosovo was to remain part of Yugoslavia since the autonomy vote was gone. So to save himself, his army, and his police who kept him in power, Milosevic agreed to NATO's terms.

Clinton officials claim the Kosovo war was a success because the Serb forces withdrew from Kosovo and 800,000 or so ethnic Albanians returned to their homes. Furthermore, the White House insists the people of Kosovo are better off today than they were when Milosevic carried out his ethnic cleansing. But critics of the war make several telling points: The administration was poorly prepared for war and naively thought a few bombing attacks would end the war; the refugee flow increased after the bombing started, and it was then that Milosevic intensified ethnic cleansing. Kosovo is not a multiethnic society as NATO promised it would be. Violence and intimidation of the remaining Serbs continue, and it has proven impossible to get Serbs and Kosovars to live together— a de facto partition has occurred in spite of KFOR and the United Nations.

Many Russians still see the Kosovo peace deal as a defeat and a capitulation to NATO. Certainly the Russian military leaders see it this way, and thus as a blow to Russian prestige. Russia was determined not to bow to NATO; it wanted the United Nations to run the peacekeeping operation and use significant Russian troops who would report to the United Nations, not to the NATO command. Viktor Chernomyrdin was accused of betrayal, not of winning a victory for Russia. Russia had condemned the bombing but failed to get it ended. The Russians, however, could not change the final agreement, only some face-saving concessions were given to them. It was Finnish president Martii Ahtisaari who made the pact finally work. The Russians had not put enough pressure on Milosevic; Ahtisaari did and won the agreement—a NATO agreement, not a Russian or UN one. A formula to save face for the Russians was thought to be necessary in order to keep them under the United Nations and not reporting to NATO.

The Russia-NATO dispute over the air attack on Serbia continued into mid-June 1999. After a peace treaty and before NATO troops arrived, the Russian troops occupied the airport outside Priština, Kosovo's provincial capital, and prevented NATO's peacekeepers from coming into the airport. The Russian paratroopers dug in to defend the airport, claiming fear of attack from the KLA. Talks in Helsinki finally worked out a role for Russian peacekeepers in the NATO-KFOR system. NATO insisted the Russians must come under its command; Moscow demanded to run its own sector. This would have meant, in effect, a partitioning of Kosovo, which many observers said had been the secret purpose of the Serbs and the Russians all along. The KLA warned that Russian troops not under NATO command would be hostile to them, and asserted that the Russians who were Serb allies were not welcome in Kosovo and would be treated as "enemy forces."

The KLA caused problems by resisting disarmament after the peace accords. Finally, however, the KLA agreed to put its arms in storage sites controlled by KFOR, over a three-month period. The refugees meanwhile continued to flow back into Kosovo, in spite of warnings about mines. Before UN officials arrived, the KLA set up civil governments wherever it could, sometimes cooperating with NATO forces, sometimes ignoring them.

UN-KFOR in Kosovo

KFOR's missions are many:

> to establish a secure environment in which refugees and displaced persons can return home in safety; to establish a secure environment in which the international civil presence can operate, a transitional administration can be established, and humanitarian aid can be delivered; to help achieve a self-sustaining secure environment which will allow public security responsibilities to be transferred to appropriate civil organizations.

The various NATO units in Kosovo are doing an excellent job in rebuilding roads, buildings, the electrical network and providing food, clothing, tents, stoves, firewood, and prefabricated houses. Mine clearing, border control, health care, also are part of KFOR's duties; in the physical area KFOR is succeeding, but in controlling crime, intimidation of Serbs, and in reconciling Serbs and Albanians, it is failing.[32]

The Security Council reaffirmed the sovereignty and territorial integrity of Yugoslavia at war's end. The UN's interim administration mission in Kosovo (UNMIK) has stated that its role is only an interim one. But UNMIK has set up customs and police posts on the international borders with Albania and Macedonia; it has collected customs charges for Kosovo while declaring the German mark the legal tender of Kosovo. The dinar of the Republic of Yugoslavia is no longer accepted freely, which outrages the Serbs, as does the UN

MAP 5   Yugoslavia and Kosovo

position that Serbs are regarded as a minority in Kosovo where they are outnumbered fifteen to one.

UNMIK head Bernard Kouchner is the executive head of government in Kosovo. He has set up a Transitional Council to administer the province and a Supreme Court to head a new judicial system. The KLA has been officially demilitarized; some of its members (3,000) are included in a police force and others in the Kosovo Protection Corps for civil work. The Serbs have reacted furiously and are accused of infiltrating paramilitaries into northern Kosovo to protect and stiffen Serb enclaves. The tension will probably continue in Kosovo even if the Milosevic government is replaced. The hatred between Serbs and ethnic Albanians is too deep to allow Kosovo to remain part of Yugoslavia or for Serbs to remain in Kosovo, except in a partitioned part of that province. This the UN and NATO refuse to accept, and so a long-term occupation as in Bosnia is inevitable.

The brutality against Serbs in Kosovo and the spread of criminal gangs from Albania have frustrated the UN and NATO efforts to establish a rule of law and a multiethnic Kosovo. After months of KFOR occupation, ethnic hatred and the desire for revenge continue. Serbs have to be protected by barbed wire and forty-five thousand NATO troops (only about 100,000 Serbs and 18,000 Roma remained in Kosovo by the end of 1999). In spite of KFOR and UNMIK civilian bureaucrats, a general atmosphere of lawlessness pervades Kosovo; murders of Serbs, burning of their houses, drug-trafficking, and car thefts by Albanian mafia gangs occur daily. Few criminals are caught; fewer still are prosecuted.

Occupation officials are stunned by the brutality of the attacks on Serbs and Roma. German troops have to protect more than two hundred Serbs in a monastery in Prizren; in Mitrovica, eight thousand or so Serbs are cordoned off by a bridge into northern Kosovo; in Priština only five hundred Serbs remain of five thousand. The KLA is thought to be behind the ethnic-cleansing campaign that has sent more than 100,000 Serbs out of Kosovo. Most of the beatings and murders appear to be directed by the Kosovo Protection Corps, formed by ex-KLA rebels. Serb houses are burned, and older Serbs are beaten and killed in the streets during daylight hours. The OSCE has recorded 348 murders, 116 kidnappings, 1,070 lootings, and 1,100 cases of arson. Most crimes are committed by teenage

boys or young men. Against thugs and criminal and vengeful Kosovars, the UN has 1,800 police officers, 4,000 fewer than requested.
As a result revenge killing, intimidation, and criminal behavior are
rampant. "Months into its mission, the United Nations has not been
able to establish a rule of law."[33] The UN teams have too few people
and too little money to control or to govern Kosovo. NATO's KFOR
units are also failing to protect Serbs and Roma.

KLA-KFOR negotiations continued through September and October 1999. The KLA did not disarm by the September 19 deadline,
which was then extended by NATO; but later in the month some
KLA fighters were incorporated into a new police service or a national
guard for disaster relief. Another new service, the Kosovo Corps, will
have about three thousand men and be allowed to carry light arms.
The UN needed to approve the force before it could be set up, and
NATO secretary-general Solana described the corps as a civilian organization for humanitarian work. Russia, of course, opposed the
plan. NATO and the UN want the rest of the KLA force to become a
civil authority, not a military body. In fact, this is what the KLA has
been doing by putting its members into local government positions.

KLA opposition to Russian involvement in KFOR reached a cli-
max in Orahovac, where the Russians were supposed to take over
from Dutch KFOR troops on August 22, 1999. After a five-day dead-
lock, the Russians retreated from a roadblock set up by the ethnic
Albanians. The KLA had supported the local people and even demanded that the Russians apologize for supporting Serb ethnic
cleansing in Kosovo. NATO has come to depend on the KLA to maintain some order in Kosovo. Yet the two parties have different agendas:
NATO recognizes Kosovo as part of Yugoslavia; the KLA does not.
Also, NATO wanted the KLA to disarm and become a civilian body.
The KLA delayed until recently giving up its heavy weapons and still
wants to be designated the only police force of Kosovo.

The OSCE and UNHR published a report in September 1999
warning of the deterioration of conditions for Serbs and Roma in

Kosovo.[34] Violence and discrimination against minorities have continued since KFOR occupied Kosovo. Serbs claim they cannot get treatment in Albanian-run hospitals or get jobs in local companies under Kosovars. An estimated 175,000 Serbs have left Kosovo, out of 200,000–225,000 there before Serb forces withdrew. Northern Kosovo harbors most remaining Serbs, but few Albanians and Turks have been able to return. Clashes between Serbs and Kosovo Albanians occurred in Mitrovica after a hundred Albanians tried to enter the Serb quarter. One hundred and eighty-four French soldiers and others were wounded in September. Belgrade is rumored to have been infiltrating paramilitary forces into the north of Kosovo to stiffen Serb resistance, to divide Kosovo, and to tie the north to Yugoslavia.

But anywhere else in Kosovo, it is difficult for Serbs to survive and they therefore have mostly fled. Three hundred and forty-eight have been killed, and the rest have been subjected to harassment, the destruction of their homes and of some Serbian historic monuments and churches. The KLA denies orchestrating ethnic cleansing of Serbs, blaming rogue elements for the killing and harassment. The KLA has appointed "mayors" and a "police force," and acts as if it is the government of Kosovo, not the United Nations under Bernard Kouchner. Only the KLA has the arms and control structure to carry out the systematic ethnic cleansing of Serbs. The KLA has continually broken its agreement (Undertaking of Demilitarization and Transformation) with NATO signed on June 21, 1999, by Hashim Thaci, the KLA commander. Thaci has violated every provision of that document, according to Michael Radu of the Foreign Policy Research Institute in Philadelphia.

Thus, NATO has failed to contain the KLA and does not appear to have a strategy to deal with it or indeed with Milosevic. The fact is that the KLA, despite NATO's promise to create a multiethnic Kosovo, is on the way to becoming a purely Albanian area under the de facto control of the KLA, an antidemocratic, violent organization.

It is doubtful, therefore, that the UN will ever achieve its goal of a multiethnic democracy in Kosovo. Revenge justifies all crimes, and those who call for pluralism are threatened and called pro-Serbian vampires. The KLA has shown a brutal authoritarian streak gained during their war against Serb forces. This authoritarianism bodes no good for a peaceful pluralism in Kosovo, and the UN or NATO is unlikely to be able to stop the violence or keep Kosovo in the Yugoslav federation.

The UN and NATO officials are, of course, worried over the de facto partitioning of Kosovo, which starts at the bridge in Mitrovica, thirty miles south of Kosovo's real border with Serbia. The northern part of Mitrovica is mostly Serb, the southern portion is Albanian, so the city is divided and the two parts are patrolled by French troops at the bridge separating the north from the south. NATO and the UN have not tried to extend their authority north of the bridge because they fear violence and frightening the Serbs.[35]

As noted earlier, the peacekeepers thus seem unable to stop this de facto partitioning of the north or to integrate Serbs and Albanians anywhere in Kosovo. A partitioned Kosovo would defeat the stated purpose of intervention in Kosovo, yet NATO has been reluctant to force the integration of North Kosovo or to stop Serb military and police from coming into the north. UN and NATO officials have allowed Serbs to concentrate where they feel safer, in effect setting up a division of Kosovo as was done in Bosnia. Officials argue that to force the opening of Mitrovica would lead to violence and to the flight of more Serbs from Kosovo. So the UN administration does little and alienates both sides. Albanians demand the right to go anywhere in Kosovo, even to the north where some Albanians and Turks used to live. Serbs, fearing revenge against them, oppose any move across the bridge into the north, and tough youth from both sides patrol the bridge area and question visitors to decide who is to be allowed in. UN efforts to staff multiethnic hospitals in the north have, therefore, failed. Albanian staff are intimidated and leave. Serbs control and police the north of the city, even threatening NATO and UN officials. Belgrade pays the salaries and pensions of officials in northern Kosovo, even when it doesn't pay officials in Serbia.

Life is therefore oppressive for all in the area; there is little electricity, the phone lines have been cut to Serbia. But food and gasoline still come across the border as do "defenders" of the Serb enclave. Serbs admit terrible things were done to Albania in the past, and they don't expect forgiveness and reconciliation. The Serbs of Kosovo intend to resist integration in Kosovo to protect themselves and over time hope to be integrated into Serbia. UNMIK head Kouchner calls reconciliation the key to peaceful integration; unfortunately, he lacks the ability to build such reconciliation or the will to take over the Serb enclaves in northern Kosovo or elsewhere.

Old hates have reignited and Albanian raiders have been hitting Serb towns since July 1999, as NATO has looked on. NATO is not actively preventing ethnic Albanian extremists from crossing over the demilitarized zone between NATO and the Serb army and even denies that such raids have occurred. In November 1999 a four-hour battle took place between raiders from Kosovo and Serbian police. A lower-intensity conflict between KLA raiders and Serb police and villagers has broken out along the 75-mile-long border between Kosovo and Toplica county in southern Serbia.[36] NATO troops on the border claim they see little or no activity, and in any case they can do little or nothing to stop the cross-border raids. Villagers in the area see these attacks as part of a broader plan by the KLA to achieve a greater Albania. The region was Albanian until 1877, when the Serbs took it from the Ottoman Empire and drove the Albanians into Kosovo. The Albanians have not forgotten this expulsion, and KLA maps show the region as one part of a greater Albania.

The Serbs, on the other hand, feel they are limited in their response to the raids from Kosovo by the military agreement that ended seventy-eight days of NATO bombing. Only a few Serb police are allowed along the DMZ. To the Serbs, NATO appears either indifferent to the attacks or supportive of them because of Serb atrocities in Kosovo. KLA headquarters in Priština denies it is organizing the attacks but admits that "uncontrolled elements" of the

KLA may be responsible. Local Serb villagers accuse the NATO-led Kosovo Protection Force (made up of ex-KLA members) either of collusion in the raids or of incompetence in stopping them. And KFOR troops did not hide their anti-Serb feelings from a *Wall Street Journal* reporter when he interviewed them.[37]

Meanwhile, Milosevic continues to rule Yugoslavia and threaten the region. The opposition in Belgrade is inept, frightened, and divided and is unlikely to be able to force Milosevic from power. Setbacks leave Milosevic unfazed; his young toughs beat up people, kill some of the opposition, and rally the people against NATO. His country has been defeated in Kosovo, bombed in Serbia, isolated from Europe, and suffers from a severe economic decline. Milosevic and his top leaders are indicted war criminals. Yet he still rules supreme and ignores the opposition.[38] No change is likely if Belgrade does not change its ruler, and there should be no aid from the West, even though that will mean no stability for Serbia's neighbors, especially in Kosovo, Macedonia, and Montenegro.

The peace agreement, therefore, has failed to address the primary cause of troubles in Kosovo and everywhere else in the Balkans — Slobadan Milosevic. There can be no real peace in the region as long as Milosevic rules in Belgrade. Disputes over details will continue and will make difficult, if not impossible, any lasting settlement in Kosovo and the region. Stubborn bloody-mindedness is a national characteristic of Serbs. Delays and compromise are likely to drive a wedge between some members of NATO and between NATO and the KLA. Add Russia to the mix, and you have a witch's brew impossible to stomach. The only solution is a change of regime in Serbia by coup, election, or resignation. It is now widely accepted that the troubles in Yugoslavia over the last ten years have been the responsibility of Milosevic; he planned the invasions and ethnic cleansing of Bosnia, Croatia, and then Kosovo, but how to replace him remains a problem.

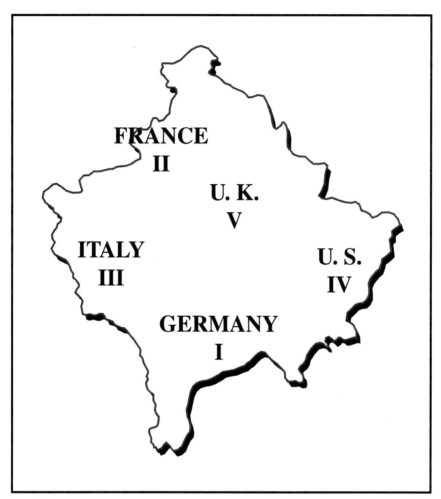

MAP 6 NATO Divisions in Kosovo

NATO after Kosovo

The air war over Serbia has created a new NATO and perhaps one with a new interventionist strategy for the future. NATO had been a defensive alliance for Western Europe, but then it bombed

Yugoslavia, a sovereign state, for mistreating its citizens in one of its provinces. This change in NATO's behavior has vast consequences for NATO and the United States. The concern is that the United States and its allies, having declared war on a sovereign state for abusing its people, may in the future try to enforce similar humanitarian standards elsewhere in Europe or in other parts of the world.

The air campaign may also mark the reemergence of Germany as an active military force involved in ensuring a safer, more peaceful Europe. For years the Germans and NATO ignored Serb aggression in the Balkans; now they are trying to stop Milosevic from doing in Kosovo what they let him do in Croatia and Bosnia-Herzegovina. Although Germany supported the air war, its Green Party opposed any use of ground troops and threatened the ruling government's coalition.

Since the end of the Cold War, NATO has been looking for a reason for its continued existence. Humanitarian intervention may become that reason. The United States pioneered interventionism in Somalia and Haiti to feed people and to restore peace and order to divided nations. In Kosovo, NATO tried to force a sovereign state, Yugoslavia, to stop mistreating its internal enemies. Although international law has said that external aggression should be resisted, no such right exists to intervene in the internal affairs of a sovereign nation. Interventionist internationalism was being defended to prevent ethnic cleansing in Kosovo. Will NATO's bombing encourage humanitarian intervention elsewhere in the future? The implications are stark. Does NATO intervene in Russia now that the Chechens have taken up arms again? Should it intervene in Africa in any of several bloody conflicts? And how about China and Taiwan or India or Indonesia?

The NATO air campaign against Yugoslavia thus posed serious challenges to NATO unity and may bring far-reaching changes in the alliance. Although the air campaign was criticized, it did bring the Serbs to the negotiating table and made them agree to a settlement; it sent the UN and NATO peacekeepers into Kosovo and has led to the return of most Kosovars to their homes. This partial success may encourage air war elsewhere against other weak but aggressive regimes.

Observers such as General William E. Odom see the Kosovo peace deal as only a truce that allows the various sides in the Yugoslav imbroglio to get ready for the next war.[39] Clinton's hesitation and failures since 1993 in the Balkans have weakened NATO and caused alarm among our European allies. They feel the United States is no longer a strong, reliable ally, and some of our allies plan to strengthen the European Security and Defense Identity (ESDI). The demise of NATO may well be one of the legacies of Clinton's presidency. U.S. global leadership and its moral leadership have also been shaken by the strategy of relying on bombing only and by failing to get rid of Milosevic. Clinton's fear of casualties in Kosovo, which a ground war would have entailed, has further weakened America's moral standing.

Ethnic intolerance is too great in the Balkans to buy a peaceful co-existence for an independent Kosovo. The Serbs will not accept ethnic Albanian rule over the sacred land of the Serbs. The only solution, then, is partition; it is unappealing, but workable and inevitable. Partition would divide Kosovo along ethnic lines permanently, and would give the Serbs the historic lands they feel are vital to them—Pec, medieval monasteries, and the field of Kosovo Polje. The KLA may not care, because it aims for a greater Albania and these Serb lands are a small portion of that dream. There are many objections to partition, but it may be the best solution to ethnic conflicts. Partition along ethnic lines should have been effected in Bosnia-Herzegovina, but Clinton opposed it. Now Croat, Serb, and Muslim live in suppressed hostility in Bosnia and wait until NATO forces leave and fighting breaks out again. The partitioning of Kosovo may, unfortunately, lead to further redrawing of borders throughout the Balkans. Serbia may want all Serbs in a Greater Serbia, which it was stopped from achieving in the 1990s. International powers may then have to govern the Balkans as they did in the late nineteenth century.

What lessons can NATO learn from this lengthy confrontation over Bosnia and Kosovo and peace negotiations with a prickly Serbia and Russia? The military in Moscow have won a political victory and an exoneration of their position that the West only respects Russian force. The Russians by their arrogance and duplicity have won a sphere of influence in Bosnia, Kosovo, and Serbia. The West should have learned, yet again, not to trust the Russians, and not to involve them in NATO activities. Even though the Cold War is over and communism defeated, things are still perceived differently in a Russia yearning after its lost superpower status.

The war in Kosovo made the Europeans realize that they needed a unified defense and security system. But while the euro (the common currency) was being promoted, the common defense and security system was neglected. The Europeans do not want to give up NATO, but they do want to have an independent defense system. The United States has dominated NATO and has the most advanced air and weapon systems, as the war in Kosovo showed. The Europeans depended on U.S. airpower, strategic reconnaissance, and laser-guided bombs, but many now seem determined to do something about it. But what? They are unwilling to spend large sums of money to catch up, even if the voters were to agree. The Greens and the left may not allow significant sums to go to arms instead of welfare. But to lessen their dependence on the U.S.-led NATO, the Europeans will have to spend large sums on restructuring their militaries. There will also have to be a redesign of the command and control of any future European Security and Defense Identity—nineteen nations operating by consensus cannot respond quickly or efficiently to war.

Today, the Europeans spend less on defense and more on welfare than does the United States. They have troops but not aircraft, advanced missiles, or transport to supply armies. For the Europeans to be free of dependence on the United States, two things are necessary: They must increase their defense spending by at least 50 per cent, and combine their defense industries and military procurement in a European security system. They are unlikely to spend much more on defense; they want a peace dividend—so they might spend even less. The new EU and the euro call for countries to cut deficits and limit public spending. Tax increases to pay for military hardware and a diversion from welfare to defense spending are therefore politically unlikely. Each nation-state will resist reorganization of its local defense industries for an ESDI system, because it would cost too much and eliminate local jobs.

There are no EU forces, only national ones in Kosovo: German, French, and British soldiers under a NATO unified command. While Prime Minister Blair has been firm on bringing peace to Kosovo and on war crimes, Britain has failed to adopt the euro and to join in the economic institutions where much of European policy is made. Germans are not anxious for military engagement, nor are the French, who suspect U.S. policies and leadership; but there is growing pressure to create and arm an ESDI.

The European Union leaders are therefore planning a rapid intervention force of 60,000 soldiers and 300 to 500 aircraft that can fight for a year or so in conflicts like the one in Kosovo this year. The proposed Anglo-French "Euro-force" is a piece of feeble posturing disdainful of America's historic role in guarding Europe's freedom, says John Keegan, defence editor of the London *Daily Telegraph*. Yet the United States shouldn't oppose this effort of the Europeans to go their own strategic way. The Europeans may not be able to construct a parallel defense to NATO, but the EU should be encouraged to do so while being cautioned not to undermine or weaken NATO.

Part V

The Future of NATO

United during the Cold War, a larger NATO, free from the threat of the USSR, was not able to act quickly to reach consensus during the 78-day air war in 1999 against Yugoslavia. In the future, in a further expanded NATO (in the Balkans and Baltics), it is even less likely to be able to find consensus and to respond quickly or even to reach agreement in case of an armed attack on its periphery or on one of its newer members. Some NATO allies may choose not to join a military response or even to man a peacekeeping force. The Greeks, for example, did not approve of NATO's bombing of the Serbs, so did not take part in the air war and angrily protested the attack on their fellow Orthodox Church members, the Serbs. For fifty years, deterrence had worked because of U.S. leadership of NATO and alliance cohesion. In the future an enlarged NATO will face problems of how and when to respond to armed attack, or whether or not to intervene in a civil war in a sovereign state.[40]

The air war in the Balkans reflected a fundamental shift in international behavior, and it did not conform with either national or international law. The UN Charter is based on the principle that the borders of sovereign states are inviolable and that the UN is a collective security system set up to prevent wars between sovereign states, not within a sovereign state. Yet NATO acted with the tacit support of the international community in attacking Yugoslavia. With the end of the Cold War, NATO and the United States felt free to attack the Serbs. The Helsinki Accords also gave NATO an excuse to intervene—all states have an interest in the way in which states treat their citizens. In the new world after the Cold War, sovereign rights are accompanied by sovereign responsibilities. International law, however, has been slow to reflect this new consensus of Helsinki. Russia and China, for example, with their own internal conflicts to resolve, oppose such outside interference. Humanitarian interventionism against sovereign states in internal wars contradicts international law. Legal scholars seem to agree that NATO action against Yugoslavia was illegal, although it was just. NATO, therefore, broke an international code that forbids interference in the internal affairs of a sovereign state; this has been an international law since the Treaty of Westphalia in 1648. But there is strong precedent for interfering in a sovereign state; it is *not* an absolute norm.

Articles IV and V of the Washington Treaty commit members to defend other NATO members against attack. After Kosovo, NATO will have to decide whether it will intervene again for humanitarian reasons in a sovereign state oppressing its citizens or in areas outside NATO membership. How to treat other threats—terrorism, biological and chemical weapons, nuclear proliferation—will also be future problems for NATO. The same elements that guaranteed NATO's effectiveness in the past will be required in the future, that is, "clarity of purpose, leadership, determination, readiness and cohesion."[41]

"De-Balkanizing the Balkans"

Southern Europe, or the Balkans, are at a political crossroads.[42] These nations want to be integrated into NATO and the European Union (EU). Governments in the region cooperated with NATO during the recent air war and suffered great economic losses, and they now expect to be repaid for their help to NATO by being admitted to it and the European Union. The governments of Bulgaria, Romania, Macedonia, Albania, and Slovakia claim to be becoming more democratic and reformist. They all need economic assistance and want the security systems of NATO or Partnership for Peace (PfP). These governments expect to join NATO in the 2003 tranche. NATO thus faces another debate over enlargement in the next few years. NATO will need to carefully study its future policies in the Balkans, the drawbacks of further enlargement, and how to deal with the Russians. To further dilute NATO with four new members might fatally weaken the Alliance's ability to respond quickly and effectively or to manage crises. Meanwhile NATO will have to station forces in Bosnia, Kosovo, Albania, and Macedonia to keep the peace.

NATO is for now committed to providing collective security for the Balkans as part of a pan-European system. This commitment was set forth in the Alliance's "Strategic Concept" at the fiftieth-anniversary meeting in April 1999. Furthermore, the "security table" for the Stability Pact for Southeastern Europe set up by the EU in Cologne in June 1999 was, in fact, given to NATO. It is clear that NATO will be the major security partner in Southeastern Europe, although the UN, the OSCE, and the EU will also play significant roles. NATO alone has the forces to secure the Balkans. At present NATO forces number 30,000 in Bosnia-Herzegovina and 57,000 in Kosovo. There are troops also in Albania and Macedonia, and troops may soon be needed in Montenegro.

In Bosnia, the Stabililization Force (SFOR) is being reduced further, by about a third of the current strength, according to the NATO defence ministers. But much work remains to be done in Bosnia: to detain war criminals, to fight corruption, to help the return of refugees to their homes, and further to reduce arms force levels and military budgets.

Other ties that link NATO to the Balkans are the 1999 Membership Action Plan (MAP) and the Partnership for Peace. The MAP was formed to reassure states not admitted to NATO in 1999 and to tell them how to prepare for admission. These guidelines not only ready states for admission, but also bind future members to NATO through defense reform and modernization efforts, much as Partnership for

Peace did for Poland, Hungary, and the Czech Republic before 1999. NATO, through MAP, will provide its members planning tools to ensure "the interoperability of their armed forces."[43] The Membership Action Plan does not, however, guarantee admittance to NATO.

Brussels now sees the Balkans as the prime threat to security in Europe in the next century. Therefore the Alliance has reshaped Partnership for Peace (24 members) and the Euro-Atlantic Partnership Council (44 members) to include the nations of the Balkans, except Bosnia-Herzegovina, Croatia, and Serbia. Partnership for Peace exercises and EAPC comparative mechanisms were expanded to the region. Another major development for Southeastern Europe was the setting up at the Washington conference of a new consultative forum of NATO, made up of NATO members and the seven states neighboring on Serbia. These efforts have created the Stability Pact for Southeastern Europe, "the major political and institutional response to the Balkans crisis."[44]

The Stability Pact, therefore, will be the primary security organization for the Balkans in the coming years, but much of the work of economic reconstruction and security guarantees will be done by other groups under the organization. For example, the Stability Pact, initiated by the EU, will be under the only pan-European body in the region, the OSCE, which is, in effect, a regional arrangement under Chapter VIII of the UN Charter. A German, Bodo Hombach, has been appointed as special coordinator for the Stability Pact; an American, Robert Barry, is the regional coordinator for Southeastern Europe. Three working groups have been set up to address such matters as the rights of minorities, issues involving refugees, border questions, means to strengthen civil society, and the role of law and good governance in Southeastern Europe. There is also a Working Table on Economic Reconstruction, Development, and Cooperation and one on Security Issues.

Countries in the region are initiating cooperative ventures to improve security and stability, such as the Royaumont Process to strengthen democracy, the Southeastern Europe Cooperation Initiative, the Southeastern Europe Defense Ministers, the Southeastern Europe Cooperation Process (for political, economic, security, and humanitarian regional cooperation), and the Organization for Black Sea Economic Cooperation.[45]

For the nations in the Balkans, only admission to NATO and the EU will provide economic development and military security as well as integration into the European community. The Balkan nations feel their cooperation in the war against Serbia and their participation in MAP and KFOR have won them the right to join NATO and the EU. They are reforming their economies and democratizing their governments. Three countries in the Baltics also expect to join NATO in the next tranche.

But this hope for admission into NATO and the EU by countries in the Balkans and the Baltics "contains strong potential for disappointment, dissatisfaction and disarray."[46] The war in Kosovo demonstrated the difficulties of fighting a war by committee, and by admitting new members NATO runs the risk of further reducing its coherence and ability to act speedily and effectively in crises. Consensus, obviously, will be even more difficult to achieve in a further enlarged NATO. Then there is the Russian problem if NATO expands into areas Russia feels are in its sphere of influence. Perhaps NATO should let the EU enlarge itself first, then, as the new members integrate themselves into the EU, develop their economies, and further democratize, NATO membership may not be as necessary. Instead, membership in the WEU, OSCE, and Partnership for Peace or in the European Security and Defense Identity (ESDI), a pan-European security system, could well be enough. In any case, conditions in Europe call for another assessment of NATO's future, such as the Harmel Report of 1967, which reorganized the goals and mission of the military alliance.

There is, of course, an economic dimension to the Balkan crisis: the need for economic growth and political stability in the region.

There the EU, not NATO, will be the biggest player, through the Stability Pact for Southeastern Europe and its Working Table on Economic Reconstruction, Development and Cooperation. To join the EU the Balkan nations will need to make the necessary economic and political reforms, aided by technological aid and advice and, of course, freer trade and free market programs.[47]

NATO in the Next Decade

The next decade will see further growth of NATO. In 1999 Poland, Hungary, and the Czech Republic joined NATO; Slovenia, Romania, and Austria are likely to be the next members early in the twenty-first century, and the Balkan and Baltic states are clamoring for admission after them. An expanding NATO will thus be opened to many more new members to build a broad European security system. NATO today has nineteen members, and Partnership for Peace has forty-three countries in its training program for future NATO membership. Not only will NATO expand, so will the European Union. And a larger EU will help produce more effective security and defense cooperation there. If the Baltic states can qualify for the EU, they need not be in NATO. Already the European Security and Defense Identity (ESDI) is developing, and this pillar of the EU can strengthen NATO but not replace it as the most important and effective security organization in Europe.[48]

The United States should welcome all of this, not resist it. A stronger EU should help the former Warsaw Pact states develop economically and stabilize politically. A strong EU will mean a stronger NATO, with plenty of resources to form rapid reaction forces and with a larger manpower pool (and a less expensive one too) for peacekeeping and nation-building forces in the troubled parts of the Balkans and elsewhere, even in the Commonwealth of Independent States. The United States, however, should insist on more burden-sharing of NATO's tasks and responsibilities with the Europeans and not always act as the leader of NATO or the sole source of high-tech warfare equipment. The WEU, therefore, should be encouraged to take on more of NATO's responsibilities and to work with the ESDI for a Europe-wide defense system backed up by NATO. Let the WEU, the Anglo-French "Euro force," OSCE, and ESDI handle most of the peacekeeping and conflict resolution functions of NATO in Europe. Activities outside Europe should also be shared if the EU wants to participate.

Peacekeeping, conflict resolution, nation building, and cooperation among nations in Europe should be more Europe's concern than the United States' in the future. Cooperation with Russia will be one of the most important tasks of NATO or the ESDI and OSCE. Institutions such as the NATO-Russia Permanent Joint Council, the Euro-Atlantic Partnership Council, and groups such as the UN, World Bank, IMF, and Council of Europe can also help integrate, stabilize, and develop Russia.

In the future, terrorism and biological, chemical, and nuclear warfare will all have to be dealt with by NATO and the Atlantic Alliance. There will also need to be solidarity among NATO members to face common challenges in the Middle East and in the gulf. A commitment to defend all the countries of Europe, whether members of NATO or not, will be necessary to ensure peace throughout Europe.

Leadership of NATO, therefore, should pass from the Americans to the Europeans early in the twenty-first century. Germany is a logical choice to take over from the United States. Fears of Germany are no longer justified. Deutsche mark nationalism has replaced German militarism for the last fifty years; now there is the euro currency to replace the deutsche mark. Germany is tied irrevocably to the West by the EU, the euro, and NATO. It has the vision of a greater Europe that neither the French nor the British have. The United States should remain a member of NATO but should share more of the military burden and leadership roles with its European allies. We need Europe and Europe needs us, and world peace is best served by a cooperating Atlantic Alliance system with fair burden-sharing of military expenses and a lesser leadership role in Europe for the United States.

The United States can rightly expect its allies to commit more to their national defense and to NATO than they do at present. American global responsibilities have required the United States to reduce its commitments to NATO (only 100,000 American troops remain in Europe), but the EU with its 350 million people and advanced economy can certainly spend more on defense and less on welfare. The Europeans seem committed to NATO now and for the foreseeable future. But leaders of the EU want to play a more independent role in foreign affairs and defense matters. As the WEU and ESDI grow and assume high-tech responsibilities and more airpower, the United States can further reduce its commitment. NATO need not be weakened by that shift in responsibilities from the Americans to the Europeans.

Europeans in recent years have been complaining about U.S. unilateralism and arrogant leadership. The French, at least since Charles de Gaulle in the early 1960s, have argued that the French or European powers should not be so dependent on the United States and should have their own independent strategic defenses. The French today accuse the United States of isolationism, capriciousness, and acting unilaterally. Several NATO allies were upset by the U.S. Congress rejecting the test ban treaty. European leaders also claim that the Americans will not accept Europe as an equal partner and too often act unilaterally, not multilaterally. European leaders call, therefore, for an independent European common foreign and defense policy. Some claim, erroneously, that the Americans don't want a multilateral defense system for Europe. The United States dominated, for example, the high-tech air war over Yugoslavia. But, in the future, the American military want the Europeans to bear a bigger share of the expenses for the defense of Europe and for peacekeeping efforts there. These issues will continue to plague NATO and the United States for some time to come in the twenty-first century.

The war in Kosovo led the Europeans to look to a more independent defense and foreign policy. President Jacques Chirac at an international conference on November 4, 1999, claimed the world is not as safe with only one superpower, the United States, as in a multipolar world in which Europe, not the United States, dominates. The United States, Chirac charged, acts too often unilaterally, and is drifting into isolationism.[49] The French, Germans, and British are concerned that the United States wants to amend the 1972 Anti-Ballistic Missile Treaty with Moscow and to build an anti-missile defense system. NATO allies believe this could destabilize the global balance of forces. Also the United States, in rejecting the test ban treaty, further angered its European allies.

The Russian military also has been taking a hard line against NATO during and since the air war against Yugoslavia. The land and air war in the breakaway region of Chechnya has led the military to call for an all-out military victory against the rebels and, ominously, has been warning Russian politicians to keep out of the way. The example of NATO bombing Yugoslavia may have encouraged the Russians to launch a brutal air and land war against the Chechens, and world opinion was unable to force the Russians to stop.

Other key issues facing NATO in the near- and long-term future are continued threats in Europe and on its borders, especially Kosovo-type incidents as well as instability in North Africa, the Middle East, and the gulf. It is not clear that, lacking forceful U.S. leadership, which some European leaders are challenging, NATO will have the will or the decision-making coherence to meet all threats inside or outside Europe. It is uncertain whether the European Union can fashion quickly a consensus to act or to select effective strategies to meet all the threats to its security. NATO may still be needed for some time.

Then there is the question of the U.S. commitment to NATO. The U.S. role in NATO is being challenged by the EU, the ESDI, and, within NATO, by France, Germany, Greece, and Italy. The United States will have to do more consulting with the Europeans to overcome these differences, just as the EU will have to increase its defense spending and reduce its welfare benefits. The U.S. dominance in high-tech warfare is resented by the allies in NATO, and the Americans will have to help the Europeans develop stronger airpower, more high-tech weapons, and more powerful military forces for ESDI for use inside and outside of NATO.

All of this depends not only on U.S. attitudes but on Europe's leadership and capabilities. Will Germany's neighbors accept German leadership of the European defense and security pillar? The United States, therefore, needs and wants a strong, stable Europe. By sharing decision making and technology, by doling out duties and responsibilities, the United States could safely reduce its NATO commitments, leave Europe to the Europeans, and focus more on other areas of the world, important to U.S. national interests. Nevertheless, the United States will have to resist strong internal forces of isolationism and unilateralism.

Because of U.S. leadership, NATO has been able to act in the Balkans and in the gulf, but other out-of-area problems will pose a threat to NATO's ability to act quickly in times of crisis. The United States therefore needs to rebuild its coalition with its allies. Then too, there are other threats that NATO has to learn to deal with: terrorism, biological and chemical warfare, nuclear arms proliferation, and vast, barely controlled immigration from poor countries to the West.

All these issues will have to be worked out in cooperation with NATO and the West's allies around the world. The United States cannot, and should not, go it alone; the United States should not play the role of policeman to the world. Nor should it withdraw to its continental borders and let the world go to hell. The United

States has national interests in Europe and elsewhere, and it is on these interests that we should concentrate.

In any case, U.S. usable power remains limited and the world a risky place; yes, we still should intervene abroad—but only where U.S. vital interests are directly threatened. When foreign statesmen describe themselves as enemies of the United States, they should be taken at their word—they are sure not to lie. The United States should take suitable counteraction. But the United States cannot eradicate evil regimes or impose its own institutions on the world at large. Such a foreign policy would make excessive demands even on the strength of the United States; such a foreign policy would more- over never gain essential domestic backing. Like it or not, the world continues to be made up of sovereign states. Between them they command a great degree of trust. American politicians cannot afford to ride roughshod abroad over such loyalties. Indeed scholar- politicians as distinguished and varied in outlook as Hans Mor- genthau, Henry Kissinger, and George F. Kennan have all shown that it is either perilous or impossible for the United States to base its foreign policy alone on the higher morality. It is beyond the power of the United States and the inclination of its people to enforce democracy from the Ukraine to Syria, the People's Republic of China to Burundi. Where necessary the United States should inter- vene but only in coalition with the UN or regional groups such as NATO; we need to cooperate with others to keep the peace.

The Pentagon has not yet come to grips with America's role as imperial policeman and peacekeeper in places like Bosnia, Iraq, and Kosovo. Extended deployments, low pay, and old stupidities of the military staff have hurt retention and recruitment rates. Morale is poor; there are shortages in advanced munitions. Part of the problem has been cuts in the budget, but most of the trouble comes from try- ing to play world policeman and a failure to face up to the new con- ditions posed by the end of the Cold War. The military needs to adapt itself to its new geopolitical position since the implosion of the other superpower, the Soviet Union. New strategies for the next war need to be developed because the armed forces will have to adapt to this new world with smaller, more rapid response units, and fewer aircraft carriers. The next war will require fewer big tanks and more high-tech ammunition and unmanned planes and weapons. In any case, NATO will remain our major instrument for conflict resolution and war-fighting initiatives in Europe. For the last fifty years NATO has been the most successful military alliance in the history of the world. Let's hope it will remain so well into the twenty-first century.

Postscript

Neo-isolationist politicians and pundits have argued that NATO failed to justify military intervention adequately or to achieve a victory in foreign policy. The war lasted longer than planned, spawned a major refugee crisis, caused massive economic and social disruption, and resulted in the death of thousands of innocent Serb civilians yet left Milosevic in power to continue destabilizing the region. The Clinton administration had little understanding of the origin of the Kosovo crisis, the complexity of the dispute, or the resolve of Serbian nationalists. The United States and NATO should have mediated a settlement as they almost did in Rambouillet and not in effect cooperated with the Kosovo Liberation Army with its greater Albanian agenda. The air war also severely damaged U.S. relations with Russia and China. All in all, the war was a failure, as is peacekeeping in Kosovo, proclaim critics of NATO.

Bosnia and Kosovo Report Card for NATO

The 1998 elections in Bosnia showed some hopeful trends toward building a multiethnic political system and a viable working national government. A national presidency, a parliament, and entity presidencies and parliaments exist in the federation, but more needs to be done to establish the rule of law, combat crime, and privatize the economy.

The International Police Task Force (IPTF) and the stabilization force (SFOR) have achieved only narrowly limited objectives. They lack the political backing to do more: war criminals move freely between Bosnia and Serbia, and although lower-level officials are occasionally arrested, high-level leaders have not yet been held accountable. This sends a bad political message, feeds insecurity, impedes refugee returns, and prevents economic restructuring. Some progress has been achieved, but much remains to be done towards civilian implementation of the Dayton Accords and the creation of a sustainable peace and a functioning state in Bosnia and Herzegovina. The large nationalist parties dominate and slow down the emerging political pluralism and multiethnic parties. Elected officials blatantly obstruct the work of SFOR, preventing the establishment of workable, common institutions of government and thwarting the return of minority refugees. The Bosnian economy has improved due partly to an increase in the number of small and medium-sized businesses but mostly because of large amounts of Western aid. Corruption and organized crime continue, however, to retard development and the growth of a civic culture. Corruption can only be limited by enforcing codes of laws and standards for government officials and by scaling down the role of the public sector. Economic growth could be fostered by privatizing state-owned assets.

In the April 8, 2000, elections, some Bosnian communities abandoned the nationalist parties of the Croat, Serb, and Bosnian Muslims, as the canton of Tuzla had done earlier. They shifted their allegiance to the opposition Social Democratic Party (formerly the Communist Party), which favors economic reforms, the return of refugees, and full implementation of the Dayton process. The Social Democratic parties did well throughout Bosnia; some multiethnic parties won in some cities, although the nationalist parties did better. The biggest victory was the defeat of the Muslim nationalist party in Sarajevo. Observers hope that these election results will lead to a backlash against the nationalist factions in Bosnia and else-where. The nationalists have shown that they cannot run the coun-try and that they are corrupt as well as inefficient. NATO and the international community, however, are reducing their forces, dis-couraged by the corruption and the inability to privatize Bosnia's heavy industry and mining operations. Much remains to be done, therefore, by the opposition to attract more Serb and Bosnian voters, if recovery is to proceed.

In Kosovo, too, NATO has run into unexpected difficulties. When the Kosovo Liberation Army was publicly disbanded in Sep-tember 1999 after NATO occupied Kosovo, it seemed that most people would soon be able to return to their normal lives. Recently, however, conflict has increased, both within the ranks of the ethnic Albanians and between ethnic Albanians and Serbs.

The former supreme commander of the KLA, Hashim Thaci, one of four members of Kosovo's interim administration, the Ad-ministrative Council, lost control of the KLA's successor, the PDK, and now leads a clan-based faction that is at odds with the PDK. The power struggle has turned murderous. Internal quarrels, score-settling, disputes over spoils and criminal fiefs, and political rivalry have left twenty-three high-ranking former KLA members dead in the year since the KLA was disbanded. In May 2000 a renowned former KLA commander and rival of Thaci, Ekrem Rexha, was shot outside his house. Another charismatic former commander, Ramush Haradinaj, stayed out of Thaci's way by limiting his power base to Prizren. He is reported to be leading Thaci in opinion polls. But the people of Kosovo are disgusted with the KLA-PDK for their in-fighting, corruption, and criminality and are equally dissastisfied with the KLA civilian offshoot—the Kosovo Protection Corps (TMK)—for its corruption, intimidation, and efforts to control the government of Kosovo. Thaci tried unsuccessfully to distance him-self from the criminal elements among the former KLA soldiers, but the people are turning away from him to support the Democratic League of Kosovo of Ibrahim Rugova, who led the peaceful resistance against Milosevic in the 1990s.

Serbs in Kosovo face an uncertain future even after the year of UN control. An estimated 567 people have been murdered since KFOR troops arrived on June 13, 1999; one-third of those were Serbs. Violence between ethnic Albanians and Serbs intensified from February 2000 onward, especially around Mitrovica and along the Serbia-Kosovo border. Serbs are shot and bombed even though KFOR provides protection and armed escorts. They (about 100,000 of them remain) have not been able to return to their homes. Some have taken refuge in enclaves north of Kosovo, but they are being attacked by ethnic Albanians who seek to reclaim the territory. The conflict has spilled over into Serbia. In March 2000, NATO was forced to conduct operations in Serbia to restrict a separatist group called the Liberation Army of Presevo, Bujanovac and Medvedja, which had been raiding towns near the Kosovo border to "protect" ethnic Albanians from Serb police. (The KLA leadership denies any links to the group.)

The KLA's successors may yet provoke a Serb response along the borderlands, and Serbia's ally, Russia, has threatened to push for the return of Serb police to protect Serbs and their holy places. With all this violence, the Serbs have lost confidence that NATO can protect them. UN administrator Bernard Kouchner claims that the UN mission has been a success at returning ethnic Albanian refugees, but much more time is needed to reconcile Serbs and Albanians. Unfortunately, these efforts to achieve a multiethnic society are likely to fail. Serbs are boycotting voter registration, withdrawing from Kosovo's civilian administration, and refusing to cooperate with UNMIK because it has brought them few benefits. Without such cooperation, Serbs will have little say in their future. But Serb leaders seem to be counting on Milosevic to return with the Yugoslav army to protect them and to force a partition of Kosovo. Yet because

KFOR and UNMIK have failed to solve the underlying political problems in Kosovo, conditions can only get worse.

NATO members are talking of withdrawing troops from Kosovo even though they may have brought this situation upon themselves by failing to provide all the forces they promised. NATO's difficulties are compounded by the EU's failure to supply more than a quarter of the personnel pledged for police and civil administration. NATO cannot count on the United States to salvage the situation. The United States has been unwilling to risk casualties, which has weakened its efforts at the risky business of peacekeeping.

More manpower is needed to recover the arms possessed by the KLA, to contain ethnic Albanian raids into Serbia, and to allow displaced people (including 100,000–150,000 Serbs) to return to their homes. KFOR may not be able to enforce a multiethnic Kosovo, but it should keep the area stable and peaceful. The Europeans need to replace the twelve thousand troops they took out of Kosovo early in 2000, and the EU must provide its full complement of police and civil administration to UNMIK to run the state and control criminal activity.

In April 2000 the Eurocorps took over as peacekeeping troops in Kosovo. The change put KFOR under the direction of Eurocorps and gave a European flavor to the peacekeeping force by making it KFOR's general staff. European troops make up 80 percent of KFOR, and the EU contributes over half of the UN budget for Kosovo this year (2000). The new commander, General Jean Ortuño, has said he will need a greater number of troops to do his work, a warning to nations thinking of withdrawing troops from KFOR. But NATO, by handing over control of Kosovo to Eurocorps, can more easily withdraw from Kosovo and leave responsibility to the corps.

Alarmed by the increasing violence and frustrated by the lack of funding and the promised UN manpower, the United States is now seeking to redefine its policy in Kosovo. Clinton seems ready to pull U.S. troops out, no matter the cost. This trend emerged when

Secretary of Defense William Cohen, in early February 2000, said that the United States was "facing mission creep." U.S. soldiers had been called on to perform police functions that they were not trained to do, then had been castigated as bullies by the Kosovars. The Clinton administration also complained that the Europeans had failed to supply enough police or administrators to run a civil government.

The United States is also uneasy with its role in Kosovo vis-à-vis Russia. It is anxious to show the Russians that NATO's presence in Kosovo is not a strategic threat to them. It does not want to run KFOR and so encourage the already growing Sino-Russian cooperation. Nor do the Europeans want to run KFOR; the Germans are especially fearful of Russia's intentions. Hence, the Europeans are unlikely to replace the Americans if the United States pulls out. If NATO goes, the Russians and Serbs will come in and refugees will flee again. A failure in Kosovo would be a disaster for NATO and the EU and would jeopardize the future of the Balkans.

American efforts to isolate and weaken Slobodan Milosevic have failed, even though he has been indicted on charges of war crimes. The EU's and NATO's diplomatic efforts to quarantine the country have also broken down—every major European country is represented in Belgrade by senior diplomats. The United States has no diplomats in Yugoslavia and will not send any until Milosevic is removed. But after the war most NATO countries returned to Belgrade feeling that the country was too important to ignore. The French and Germans issued foreign visas for European parliamentary meetings even to those Serbs barred from traveling in the West.

Unfortunately, the United States and the EU often differ in strategy. The United States wants sanctions, while the EU wants trade and openness to weaken Milosevic. The United States has opposed the EU policy on the grounds that it creates the impression that the world has accepted that Milosevic has survived and remains in power despite NATO's efforts.

The United States and its NATO allies continue to be divided by conflicts over defense strategy. Currently the United States is considering deployment of a limited national missile defense system. The 1972 antiballistic missile treaty between Russia and the United States forbids national deployment of such a system. If President Clinton decides to deploy the system, he will need to get Russia to amend the treaty. He needs to persuade the Russians that the threat from rogue nations justifies such an amendment. The United States' European allies fear that a purely American system would not protect them, but they oppose a universal defense system that would cover China as well as rogue states. They would prefer to be included in a more limited protective system. Unless the United States involves its European allies in formulating its strategy, it risks a rift with them.

Meanwhile, Russia and Yugoslavia continue to test NATO, and China, to criticize intervention and the air war. They are planning to try to make NATO live up to the agreement it forced on Yugoslavia in 1999, which would permit Yugoslav police and troops to return to Kosovo, causing chaos among Kosovars. If NATO refuses to let the Serbs return into Kosovo, one of their provinces, NATO will be condemned internationally for violating the agreement. Milosevic is beefing up his armed forces—73 per cent of the national budget goes to his army and police forces. Milosevic and his generals have threatened to return to Kosovo in June 2000 to guard cultural sites and the Yugoslav border with Kosovo and to clear minefields. This is a typical Milosevic ploy to stir up nationalism in order to distract attention from serious domestic problems. But the reemergence of Russia and China in Yugoslav diplomacy raises the stakes considerably. General Leonid Lvaslov said Russia will force NATO to comply with its obligations and will not leave Kosovo. And the Serb and Russian governments are calling for greater military cooperation and weapons supplies. All this posturing puts both the United States and NATO in an awkward position—complying with or breaking an agreement and accepting a de facto partition of Kosovo or imposing a multi-ethnic state neither Serbs nor Albanians want.

Kosovo: The Way Out of the Quagmire

The Kosovo campaign demonstrated a long-standing problem within NATO—the United States contributed more than its share to NATO during the Cold War and it continues to do so.[50] In Kosovo the United States flew two-thirds of the air missions and launched all the precision-guided missiles because the Europeans lacked air-power and high-tech equipment and could not fly in risky situations. The assignment of 6,500 United States troops and their support staff to the Balkans harmed United States military readiness elsewhere and led Congress to seek a time limit on deployment of U.S. forces in Kosovo and Bosnia. NATO, however, wants more troops as trouble builds in southeast Serbia and Montenegro.

In the interests of both the United States and Europe, NATO needs a new "grand bargain."[51] The Europeans should modernize their armed forces, reduce the technological gap with the United States, and spend more on defense—at least 3 per cent of their GDP. In return, the United States should give the Europeans more responsibility for the defense of Europe and more operational control in NATO's command structure; for example, Europeans should run the Southern Command at Naples, NATO's Rapid Reaction Force, and other regional commands.

The EU should also provide more soldiers and civilians to the peacekeeping forces in the Balkans. It could exercise these increased responsibilities through wider use of the Combined Joint Task Force (CJTF) discussed on pages 79–80. Use of the CJTF would allow the United States to decrease its forces and slow down American over-commitment around the world. The CJTF would reduce NATO dependence on United States airpower and high-tech equipment, and would replace expensive, highly trained American soldiers with less-expensive troops from the EU. This, after all, is supposed to be a peacekeeping operation; it should not require troops trained for combat. Unfortunately for NATO, the EU will likely need troops in the Balkans for years. Sectarian hatreds have not been lessened by NATO intervention; Milosevic is still in power and is stirring up trouble in Montenegro, Macedonia, and Kosovo. The Balkans will probably remain a problem for some time, but a EU problem, not a U.S. one. The CJTF can replace NATO and can deal with flare-ups as they arise. In case of war, the advanced components and airpower of the United States could return to help defeat Milosevic.

But the United States should not withdraw from NATO because of the Bosnia and Kosovo imbroglio; the Americans are indispensable to NATO and to the peace and security of Europe. Europe cannot go it alone in defense matters. The newly promulgated European Security and Defense Identity will take years and vast sums of money to match American might. But if NATO has a more equitable burden-sharing system, and modernizes by having smaller, more mobile forces, and if the EU develops a better air force and revitalized ground forces to work in ESDI or with the CJTF, NATO should be able to meet the challenge of the future as well as it did those of the past.

One year after the war in Kosovo it is possible to consider winners and losers. The big winners were the ethnic Albanian refugees who have returned to Kosovo and have been helped to rebuild many of their homes and businesses. The big losers were the Serbs (200,000) who had lived in Kosovo before the war but have mostly fled since the Kosovars returned, except in Mitrovica and a few other enclaves. KFOR cannot stop the ethnic cleansing of Serbs in Kosovo, nor can it prevent the KLA surrogates from attacking Serbs in southeastern Kosovo. The Kosovars are now the domestic power in Kosovo; the UNMIK does not have enough personnel to govern or to police the province.

NATO has also failed to break the will or power of the Serbs. President Milosevic survived his defeat, has kept the rest of Belgrade's domain under his control, and wants a partitioned Kosovo, which both NATO and the UN are pledged to resist. Opposed to Milosevic are most of the ethnic Albanians, led by the successors of the Kosovo Liberation Army. NATO has unwillingly empowered them and appears unable to stop them from controlling Kosovo. They are determined to set up an independent Kosovo, which could expand into a greater Albania. Neither the Europeans nor the Serbs want to see this, but NATO may not be willing to prevent it. The Serb army, unharmed by the air war, will certainly try to partition Kosovo. So NATO stands opposed to both Kosovar and Serb ambitions but, at present, lacks the power to enforce its will. Unfortunately, a long period of occupation to keep the peace seems inevitable for the EU and NATO.

The war against Yugoslavia has set a legal precedent and cost a great deal politically and diplomatically. The precedent was the first case in NATO's fifty-year history of unilateral intervention against a sovereign state fighting a civil war. The costs resulted partly from NATO's numerous mistakes in the air war and partly from NATO's failures to unseat Milosevic, control its KLA allies, and establish a just and effective civilian administration after the war.

In the air war, a United States–dominated NATO sent more than a thousand aircraft on 38,000 sorties at a cost of billions of dollars, but the high-altitude bombing left Serb military and police and their defenses unharmed. The air campaign harmed Serb infrastructure somewhat but devastated trade and transportation in Yugoslavia and on the Danube and thus severely damaged Balkan states economically. The worst mistakes of the NATO air war were the killing by accidental bombing of more than twelve hundred civilians and damaging the Chinese embassy. The bombing left Serb civilians angry and the Chinese outraged, a major diplomatic blunder. The Chinese have become major supporters of Milosevic through loans and diplomacy.

After the war KFOR had three missions: to ensure safety, to enforce compliance with the cease-fire agreement, and to assist the UNMIK in its civilian function of governing, policing, and reconstructing Kosovo. Reconstruction has been ongoing, in Kosovo as in Bosnia, at a cost of several billions and much more to come. The KLA, however, only slowly disarmed and disbanded, has kept a stranglehold on power, and secretly directs ethnic cleansing and efforts to expand Kosovo's land into Serbia. Riots, killings, attacks on KFOR forces and Serb civilian leaders continue. KLA surrogates and successors have flourished in the power vacuum created by the UN's failure to set up a civil administration. Meanwhile Kosovar-controlled smuggling, criminal gangs, and the drug trade have destabilized Kosovo and Europe. Eighty percent of Europe's heroin comes through the these organizations to be distributed by the 500,000 Kosovars who live in Western Europe.

NATO's dilemmas, thus, are many: prevent partition, control the Kosovars, and restart the economy. Whereas the EU members have failed to provide enough civilian administrators and police to govern and police Kosovo, NATO has not sent enough troops to control Kosovo and the border with Yugoslavia. Pressure to pull out will increase in Europe and the United States. Withdrawing is not on the cards, but is there the will to send sufficient troops to ensure peace and stability not just in Kosovo and Bosnia but in the entire Balkan area?

Bibliographic Notes

1. David P. Calleo, *Atlantic Fantasy: The United States, NATO, and Europe* (Baltimore: John Hopkins Press, 1970), pp. 27–28.

2. Elisabeth Barker, *The British between the Superpowers, 1945–50* (London: Macmillan, 1983), p. 127.

3. Thucydides, *The Pelopponesian War*, p. 424.

4. Robert W. Clawson and Glenn E. Wilson, "The Warsaw Pact, USSR, and NATO: Perceptions from the East," in Lawrence S. Kaplan and Robert Clawson, eds., *NATO after Thirty Years* (Wilmington, Del.: Scholarly Resources, 1981), p. 114.

5. William Park, *Defending the West: A History of NATO* (Boulder, Colo.: Westview Press, 1986), p. 26.

6. A. J. Nichols, "European Integration and the Nation State: Thoughts on the 1950's," *Contemporary European History*, vol. 2, part 3, Nov. 1993, p. 285.

7. Melvyn B. Krauss, *How NATO Weakens the West* (New York : Simon and Schuster, 1986).

8. Stanley Kober, "Strategic Defense, Deterrence, and Arms Control," *Washington Quarterly*, Winter 1987, pp. 123–52.

9. Colonel Wilfred L. Ebel, "The French Republic," *Military Review*, Aug. 1979, p. 50.

10. Charles C. Moskos, "Success Story: Blacks in the Army," *Atlantic Monthly*, May 1986, p. 67.

11. Jonathan Clark, "The Conceptual Poverty of U.S. Foreign Policy," *Atlantic Monthly*, vol. 272, no. 3, Sept. 1992, p. 57.

12. L. H. Gann, ed., *The Defense of Western Europe* (London: Croom Helm, 1987).

13. John Lewis Gaddis, *The United States and the End of the Cold War: Implications, Reconsiderations, Provocations* (New York: Oxford University Press, 1992), p. 101.

14. Beatrice Heuser, "The Development of NATO's Nuclear Strategy," *Contemporary European History*, vol. 4, part 1, March 1995, pp. 37–66; Stanley Kober, "Strategic Defense Deterrence and Arms Control," *Washington Quarterly*, Winter 1991, pp. 123–51.

15. For a good summary of NATO's organization and doctrine, see Frederic N. Smith, "The North Atlantic Treaty Organization: A Brief Description," *Defense and Foreign Affairs Handbook 1989* (Alexandria, Va.: International Media Corporation, 1989), pp. 1287–94; and P. Duignan and L. H. Gann, *The United States and the New Europe, 1945–1993* (Oxford: Blackwell, 1994), pp. 253–69.

16. Helmut Schmidt, "Defense: A European Viewpoint. Europe's Contribution Should Not Be Seen Only in Terms of Military Spending," *Europe*, Nov. 1986, pp. 13–14, 45.

17. Richard F. Staar, "Soviet Arms Out of Control," *New York Times*, Aug. 19, 1991, p. 11.

18. Graham Allison, "Nuclear Objectives," *Financial Times*, Jan. 31, 1992, p. 8.

19. "The Indivisibility of Arms Control: Saving the CFE Treaty," *Atlantic Council Bulletin*, vol. 6, no. 9, Sept. 14, 1995, p. 1.

20. Alfred Cahen [formerly Secretary-General of WEU], "The Western European Union (WEU) and NATO: Strengthening the Second Pillar of the Alliance," Washington: Atlantic Council of the United States, Occasional Paper, 1990, p. 33.

21. "After Communism," *The Economist*, Dec. 3, 1994, p. 27.

22. Pat M. Holt, "NATO Must Think First before Expanding East," *Christian Science Monitor*, Jun. 1, 1995, p. 19.

23. Benjamin S. Lambeth, "Russia's Wounded Military," *Foreign Affairs*, Mar.–Apr., 1995, p. 98.

24. Rep. Lee H. Hamilton, *Christian Science Monitor*, Sept. 28, 1995, p. 19.

25. See the article by General Klaus Neumann in *NATO Review*, no. 1, Spring 1998, pp. 10–17.

26. Richard F. Staar, "Russia and the West: Changing Course," *Mediterranean Quarterly*, vol. 11, no. 4, Fall 1993, pp. 63–79.

27. Kim R. Holmes, "US-European Strategic Bargains: Old and New," Heritage Lectures, no. 627, Nov. 13, 1998, p. 2.

28. For an excellent summary of the issue, see William E. Odom, "Maintaining Status Quo Spells Death for NATO," Hudson Institute Briefing Paper, Aug. 1997, pp. 3–4.

29. "Penance for Yalta," *Wall Street Journal*, Mar. 27, 1998, p. A14.

30. See Peter Beinart, "TRB from Washington: Strange Allies," *New Republic*, Mar. 23, 1998, p. 6.

31. See Lamberto Dini, "New NATO Allies Are Boon and Drag for U.S.," *Christian Science Monitor*, Apr. 1, 1998.

32. See NATO's KFOR Press Updates on http://www.kforonline.com.

33. See Jeffery Fleishman, "Crimes, Ethnic Hatred Seething in Kosovo," *San Jose Mercury News*," Nov. 18, 1999, p. 19A, for an eyewitness account.

34. "Kosovo/Kosova as Seen as Told: The Human Rights Findings of the OSCE Kosovo Verification Mission, 1999." www.OSCE.org/Kosovo/reports.

35. Steven Erlanger, "Fears Grow over the De Facto Partition of Kosovo," *New York Times*, Nov. 14, 1999, p. 1.

36. See article in *Wall Street Journal*, Dec 14, 1999, A11.

37. Ibid.

38. See Steven Erlanger, "Ignoring Scars, Milosevic Is Stubbornly Pressing On," *New York Times*, Oct 31, 1999, p. 10.

39. See William E. Odom, "A Conditional Surrender," *New York Times*, Jun. 6, 1999.

40. See BBC News, Jun. 15, 1999, item by Jonathan Eytal.

41. Marten V. A. Heuven, *NATO in 2010* (Washington, D.C.: Atlantic Council of the U.S., 1999), p. 9.

42. Ibid., p. 10.

43. For an excellent analysis of the problems in the Balkans, see Andrew V. Pierre, *De-Balkanizing the Balkans: Security and Stability in Southeastern Europe* (Washington, D.C.: United States Institute of Peace, 1999).

44. See Pierre, *De-Balkanizing the Balkans*, p. 12.

45. Ibid., p. 13.

46. Ibid., pp. 13–14.

47. Ibid., pp. 15–16.

48. Ibid., pp. 18–19.

49. See *NATO in 2010*, p. 20.

50. See John C. Hulsman, "Kosovo: The Way Out of the Quagmire," *Backgrounder* (Heritage Foundation, Washington, D.C.), Feb. 25, 2000.

51. See John C. Hulsman, "A Grand Bargain with Europe: Preserving NATO for the 21st Century," *Backgrounder* (Heritage Foundation, Washington, D.C.), Jan. 24, 2000.

Index

Western European Military Supply Board, 11
Western Union, 12
West Germany. *See* Federal German
  Republic
WEU (Western European Union): Combined
  Joint Task Force for defense of, 60; coopera-
  tion between ESDI and, 61; limited Gulf
  War participation by, 54; NATO and future
  role of, 53–56, 119; origins of, 2; Yugoslavia
  crisis and, 69. *See also* Europe
Wilson, Harold, 37
Working Table on Economic Reconstruction,
  Development, and Cooperation, 116, 118
"Work Plan" (NACC), 59
World Federation of Trade Unions, 27
World War II: German military following,
  35–36; lessons learned by U.S. military

from, 40; state of French army following,
  33–34
World War I (The Great Patriotic War), 49

Yalta sellout (1946), 71, 72
Yeltsin, Boris, 46, 94
Yugoslavian breakup (1990s): condition of
  successor states after, 87–92; ethnic cleansing during, 86; events preceding, 85–86; international cleavages exposed by, 86;
  NATO division over, 85; WEU ineffective
  response to, 69. *See also* Bosnian crisis;
  Kosovo

Zentrale für Heimatdienst (think tank), 7
Zhirinovsky, Vladimir, 72

DATE DUE

|2/1|		

DEMCO